JWalker 95

Looking down Beach Road, circa 1905.

OLD NEWQUAY

BY

S. TEAGUE HUSBAND.

ILLUSTRATIONS BY A. A. GOLDING.

I have had playmates, I have had companions,
In my days of childhood, in my joyful schooldays—
All, all are gone, the old familar faces.

(Charles Lamb).

DYLLANSOW TRURAN

This facsimile edition of the original
published in 1985 by
Dyllansow Truran
Trewolsta, Trewirgie, Redruth, Cornwall

© 1985   Dyllansow Truran

PUBLISHER'S NOTE

Old Newquay was originally published with eleven line drawings. This new edition has been extended by the inclusion of a number of photographs provided by the Newquay Old Cornwall Society, many of which were taken in the early part of the twentieth century. Although the book describes Newquay as it was in the nineteenth century, most of the backgrounds in the photographs would have changed very little for fifty years or more.

Readers of the book will find it an interesting exercise to relate the text to some of the photographs, for example, the significance of the brief caption to the photograph entitled 'The fishermen associated with Unity Cellar' will become more apparent after reading pages 13 and 15. The publisher would welcome comments from readers who are able to add to the information provided in the captions and which is not enlarged upon in the text.

Printed and bound in Great Britain
by A. Wheaton & Co. Ltd, Exeter
ISBN 0-907566-86-3

IN

MEMORY

OF

W. H. (1817–1901)

AND

M. A. H. (1824–1914).

OLD NEWQUAY
(West).

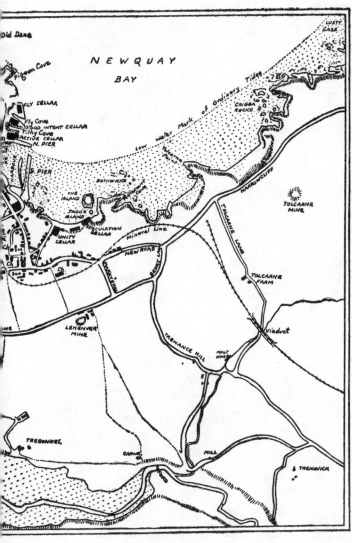

OLD NEWQUAY
(East).

CONTENTS.

LIST OF ILLUSTRATIONS.

PREFACE

This book has been written not as a guide-book to Newquay and District but to give, as far as possible, a picture of life as I knew it more than sixty years ago.

As a native of the old town I confess that it is not without regret that I have seen the old life of the place pass away and as my contemporaries have become fewer and fewer with the passing of the years I have felt impelled to take up the task of making a record of life in the old town.

Moreover some of the guide-books make statements which are both untrue and ridiculous. In one book it is said that Newquay was a collection of squalid mud huts. Such statements can be refuted only by a description of Newquay written by one who lived in it.

To this end I have done my best to verify my statements and have, wherever possible, checked my own recollections by accounts given to me by almost everyone in Newquay whose Newquay ancestry enabled them to know a great deal concerning the old conditions.

To all who have helped me in this way I offer my heartiest thanks for their kindness in answering my inquiries.

Especially must I mention Miss Michell, Mr. Edward Ennor, Mr. C. Bellingham, Mr. J. Bassett Williams, of St. Columb Minor, and Mr. Cotton Jenkin.

For facts concerning the period previous to that within my own recollection I have had descriptions given me by my parents and grandparents, and I also acquired some interesting facts from the late Mr. T.-Pappin and others of his generation.

S. Teague Husband
1923.

OLD NEWQUAY

CHAPTER I

OLD NEWQUAY

I T would be difficult to find a town more pleasantly
situated than Newquay, and in very few districts can
be seen such a diversity of scenery in so small a compass.

Modern Newquay has spread over a V-shaped peninsula
which is between the Gannel and the Atlantic. The arms
of the V are the two headlands—East Pentire, and Towan or
Newquay Headland, generally known as *the* Headland.

Between these headlands is Fistral Bay, entirely unshel-
tered and receiving the full force of the W. and N.W. gales.
From the east side of the Headland is a magnificent sweep of
cliffs around Newquay Bay to Trevose. This curve of preci-
pitous coast is varied not only in the colouring of its hard
slate rock, but it is relieved from monotony by the series of
headlands, between which are sandy beaches, differing among
themselves to such an extent, that to know one is not to know
all.

Many of these beaches lead inland into valleys with
their little streams, but the streams have not a sufficient
volume to carry any perceptible amount of mud, so that the
sand is not darkened, neither is the sea discoloured. Of
these streams only Porth and Mawgan can be called rivers.

South of the peninsula is the Gannel, an estuary
extending about two miles above Crantock Bay, into which it
flows. This sheltered stretch, sandy and scored by its small
stream at low water, but filled to form a salt water lake at
high tide, is a splendid contrast to the wild headlands and
Fistral on the seaward side, and the beautiful blue bay of
Newquay with its border of many coloured cliffs.

OLD NEWQUAY FROM MOUNT WISE

The surface of the peninsula is bare of trees,but the soft perennially green turf of the headlands diversified with the blushes of pink and purple caused by the sea pinks and heather, each in their season, make up for the lack of more luxuriant tree growth by the uninterrupted view in every direction.

From the top of Trethellan Hill broad views are obtained of coast and sea on the one side, and the Gannel on the other, beyond which farm land, wooded valleys, and moorland can be seen far into the interior.

Trees are found in all the sheltered valleys such as Trenance and Penpol, and many more spots might have been rendered beautiful in this way. Unfortunately modern Newquay has despoiled the district of many trees it once possessed and could ill spare, and has added nothing of equal beauty to take their places.

Such are the general features of this favoured district, and he must certainly be an exacting person who cannot at all times and in all weathers find a spot which will not delight him.

In one respect, at least, this general description must be amplified.

Before the new town began to grow and scatter its modern houses haphazard over the peninsula, a large expanse of blown sand spread from Fistral to the western side of the old town, coming beyond the mineral line as far as the old Baptist Chapel. The prevailing westerly winds had caused the sands of Fistral to invade the land over the low cliff and this stretch similar to Crantock Green was an undulating expanse, partly covered with the stiff marram grass near the sea, but further inland more pasture-like yet still incapable of cultivation on the Fistral side of Tower Lane. This outer area was given over entirely to sheep runs.

On the Newquay side of the lane were cultivated fields, but the soil was sandy and showed its wind-blown origin. There were sand pits in the Bark House field, and between the mineral line and the Baptist Chapel were the Commons with the Cannon Pit. The sand from these pits was used for

OLD NEWQUAY FROM ROAD UNDER THE BEACON

sanding the kitchen floors in the cottages. At the present time the golf links alone show the character of what was then a much larger area.

Old Newquay was built almost entirely between the curve of the mineral line and the edge of the cliff. It extended from the Pump House which stood fifty yards or so east of the bottom of Marky's Hill, out to the harbour.

The road from Newquay led up Marky's Hill, down Berry Road, and along the Narrowcliff to St. Columb Minor. There was only a pathway through the fields from the foot of Marky's Hill to the bottom of Berry Road, the new road, East Street, not having been made then.

"Marcus" Hill is a curious instance of a mis-applied name. It really has nothing whatever to do with the author of the famous "Meditations"!

In the district lived one Mark Cardell, who, in a fit of madness, cut his throat and was seen to go down the hill, across the field into the sea.

After that event the hill was known as Marky's Hill and, when we were young, very few of us would go alone up the hill after dark.

Beyond the harbour on the Headland side was the Deer Park with a few houses, but the town might be said to have terminated at the Red Lion.

The houses were built on either side of the main road, which curved round, following more or less the trend of the cliff. From the Old Inn (now the Central) the road to the Red Lion was called Quay Road, while the road to Marky's Hill was known as "over in town." The two Gover Lanes led down to the beach so that the Old Inn was at the focus of the town.

Outlying places were Mount Wise, with a few mine buildings, while still further away were the farms of Trenance, Carne, Tregunnel, and Pentire.

CHAPTER II

FISTRAL

O N descending from the sandy top of the low cliff to the present beach at Fistral the first thing claiming our attention is the long raised beach which extends the whole length of the cliff.

Our life is so short, compared with the length of time represented by geological changes, that it is difficult indeed for us to realise that conditions were once very different from what they are now, and that great changes have occurred in the relative levels of land and sea. There is, however, a mass of evidence to show that such has been the case.

The raised beach here, provides an example. It is easy to see that the old beach consisted of boulders, sand, and broken up shells, covered with a layer of blown sand, and there is every reason to suppose that, at some far distant period, the land stood at a much lower level than at present. At that period there was perhaps a low cliff further back toward Tower Road, and the Headland was much lower out of the water than it is now. The old beach was strewn with sand and boulders worn from the cliff, and, as the amount of sand became larger, a blown sand dune slowly grew up under the influence of the on-shore wind. A similar extent of blown sand can be seen at Crantock and on an even larger scale at Perran.

After a great length of time the land rose out of the sea, which receded a considerable distance, and the blown sand crept out after it.

Next we must imagine the land to be comparatively stationary, so that the sea began to cut back into the blown sand and underlying beach until at last the slate rocks were exposed at the base of the cliff as we see it to-day.

Looking at the beach now, it is very difficult to imagine the number of huge round white spar boulders that nestled under the cliff along the length of the beach when I was a child. They extended out on the beach for about a dozen yards, and formed a natural breakwater against the inroads of the dashing groundswell. What a source of enjoyment those boulders were to us when children !—the memory even to-day is sweet. How time slipped on as we jumped from them, or over them or on to another at some distance. Alas ! there is no such fun for the children of to-day. And why ? Because someone, who knew little of natural break-waters or their uses, suggested the breaking up of the boulders for making roads.

The same order was given for a similar breakwater of boulders under the cliff, on the Town Beach. What was the result ? The sea so encroached on the road, that a sea wall had to be built to protect it.

At Fistral the result was somewhat different. The cliffs there are composed of calcareous consolidated sand, and the action of rainwater containing carbon dioxide, which it has dissolved from the air, caused the softer parts to dissolve away, leaving many queer-shaped holes. These curious cylindrical cavities, some of them two or three feet in dia-meter, stood up like little towers perfectly round and hollow and three or four feet high; along the base of the cliff. Some had loose sand in them, while others were empty. Some were of a fantastic shape at the top, but all were equally fascinating to our childish minds. What hours of enjoyment they gave us ! One we named " the pulpit," another " the lady's boudoir." Then there was the corridor leading from one tower to the other. Yes, and I think we actually imagined they were the homes of the Pixies or fairy spirits ; but nothing of them now remains to be a source of pleasure to the hundreds of children who frequent the beach in summer.

There are a few vestiges left round, and beyond Little Fistral, but nothing equal to those on Fistral Beach.

Beautiful seaweed can still be found in the early summer for pressing on paper. I have some fine specimens obtained from Crantock and Fistral beaches.

Shells, too, are plentiful—Cowries, Wentletraps, Tapes, Rissoas, and many others. In some years during the summer months the rare and beautiful shells, Helix Janthina, have been washed ashore on Fistral Beach. They are supposed to be "waifs" of the Sargasso Sea, and are washed by the Atlantic Drift Current to this country.

Some years ago Charles Norrington, Esq., and members of his family, visiting at Glendorgal, were fortunate enough to pick up a hundred and fifty on Fistral Beach. Mr. Henry Hicks also found a considerable number, and Miss Hicks gave me two. They are a very fragile shell, of a violet-purple colour. When they are washed in in large numbers the purple stain from their bodies marks the line of high-water for several days. It was from this shell-fish, anciently found in large numbers on the eastern shores of the Mediterannean that the celebrated Tyrian dye was extracted.

CHAPTER III

SEAFARING

THOSE who have known Newquay only during the last fifty years can have no conception of life there in pre-visitor times. Moreover, the guide books, among their many erroneous statements, contrive to give an entirely false picture, both of the old town and mode of life of the inhabitants.

A century ago the town must have contained not fewer than five hundred people and the principal occupations were seafaring, with its subsidiary boat-building industry, fishing and farming.

Now-a-days one sees one or two schooners in the harbour very occasionally, but most of the craft consist of sailing and rowing boats. Formerly there would often be a dozen or more schooners in the harbour, making it a scene of activity incredible to the modern visitor.

The boats took away principally iron ore from the Perran district, and grain from all the surrounding country. The ore was brought in wagons and carts and shot through the trap doors, relics of which can be seen in Quay Hill in the wall overlooking the yards below.

Often the heap of ore would reach up to the trap door. From the base of the heap rail lines ran on to the quays as they do now, and rail wagons were loaded with ore at the heaps and run out along the quays to the vessels. The quays were of insufficient length to accommodate all the boats and those awaiting their turn were pulled up on the sandy beach within the harbour.

China clay was also shipped, but before the railway was built all the clay came in huge wagons from St. Dennis and the amount brought to the harbour was much less than in recent times.

Incoming vessels brought coal, guano and bone manure, limestone and salt. The salt was used for salting pilchards, and the limestone was burnt in the kilns in the district. One kiln was situated at the bend of the road going down the South Quay Hill. Another was near Quay House. The former was always alight.

The granary was situated where Pendrelan now stands, overlooking Slip Cove. Friday was the day when the grain was brought in by the farm wagons. On that day Red Lion Square was a scene of considerable liveliness. The vessel to be loaded was drawn up close under the cliff and the grain shot from the granary through square wooden shutes into the hold, but later it was loaded in sacks because of the danger due to shifting cargo.

Newquay people owned and captained a dozen or more schooners. It was the custom that the ownership of one quarter of the shares of any vessel carried with it the right of captaincy, provided the seamanship of the person was adequate to the post. Each boat carried five or six persons including the captain, and there were quite a number of sea-faring people among the population, not fewer than a hundred.

In addition to these a number of men were connected with the working of the boats ; hobblers who discharged and loaded the vessels, and piloted boats in and out of the harbour.

Ship-building, boat-building, repairing and sail-making gave employment to a number of men. The boats were built for Newquay owners. There were three yards. One was situated in the cove within the harbour under the Retreat. Another occupied Giant's Cove, at the Island end of the Town Beach. This cove was sheltered by a breakwater built from the cliff near the path to the Island Estate, and the large rock called Jago's Island. I remember three boats being built there. Eventually an exceptionally high tide washed away the greater part of the breakwater, and also carried off the keel of a new vessel just laid down. The keel was laid again in the ship-building yard in the Gannel ; this yard was situated just below Tregunnel.

Sail-making was carried on in the lofts in various parts of the town.

Though there had been various projects for the making of a harbour from such an early date as 1439, yet nothing was done apparently for nearly two hundred years. Carew, writing in Queen Elizabeth's time, says:—

" Neyther may I omit Newe Kaye, a place on the north coast of this hundred, so called because in former times the neighbours attempted to supplie the defect of Nature by Art in making there a Kay for the Rode of Shipping which conceyt they still retain, though want of means in themselves or the place have left the effect in nubibus."

However, Thomas Stuer applied for leave to erect a pier at Newquay in 1615, so that there was probably a short one-arm pier when Lomax bought the estate in 1830. He commenced to build the now existing South Pier, but died in 1837 before its completion.

Treffry, who bought the estate, completed the South Pier in 1838, and commenced the North Pier shortly afterwards.

Before the piers were built the vessels sheltered in the coves and were pulled up on the sandy beaches at high water so that at low water they were loaded and unloaded from carts which were drawn up alongside the vessels. The earliest harbour was a natural one—the well-sheltered Slip Cove—which is within the present harbour.

In various places around the coast are seen iron rings and S-hooks, leaded in the rocks. These were no doubt used for mooring vessels. Some were regularly used in this way. Occasionally vessels became stranded in unusual places, and these rings and hooks were put in rocks near at hand, to allow the vessel to be moored to prevent damage from heavy seas. Vessels run in on smuggling ventures would account for some of the rings in unlikely situations.

The dangers of seafaring did not allow our town to escape and we often knew what it meant to have our men in the prime of life snatched from amongst us.

Nancy Glanville's husband had built a sailing boat and had gone with his only son to test her sailing qualities. In rounding the Headland on their way back to the harbour the boat was overturned by a sudden squall and both were drowned. Nancy was left with five little girls—a truly terrible problem to confront a widow ; but like many another woman in similar circumstances, she worked and accomplished the herculean task of rearing her family.

One evening the news came that Captain Will Clemens' vessel was wrecked, and he and all the crew drowned. How well I remember the cry of agony from that household of six girls and a boy ! I never understood the full meaning of the word orphan before that sad event when the eldest daughter cried " We are orphans !" Their mother, a very delicate woman, had died not long before, and the eldest child, a girl of sixteen, took the terrible responsibility of mothering the family, and well indeed did she bring them up. Eventually the boy sailed his own vessel, two of the daughters married captains of vessels, and the youngest married a well-to-do farmer.

Another woman, whose husband was captain of a trading vessel, was left with five children. He died from injuries received on board when only forty years of age. His widow fought and overcame her difficulties, and the following incident shows she was a woman of spirit. One day a lady called to see her and said, among other things, " But, Mary, you don't seem poor. Your little family are clean and their clothing whole !" " Yes," sharply replied Mary, " and always will be while I have three-halfpence—a penny to buy soap and a halfpenny for thread."

This gives us an idea of the undaunted way our women met their troubles and conquered them.

Two of these women opened little general shops in the front rooms of their cottages. Another set up for laundry work in her house, and yet another bought a mangle with her little savings. The true sympathy of the community went out toward them and their neighbours gave them all the help they could, but there was no sinking of the Cornish spirit of independence.

Chapter IV

FISHING

THE huge shoals of pilchards and herrings, which visited the bay in former times, were a source of considerable revenue.

The pilchards came early in Autumn after the corn harvest, to be followed soon after by the shoals of herrings. Herring fishing was of far less importance than pilchard, for while only the regular fishermen were concerned with the capture of herring, a very large number who ordinarily pursued other occupations left their work and devoted their whole time during the season to the capture, curing, and exportation of the pilchard.

The immense shoals of pilchards come up the Atlantic towards the Bristol Channel but on their northward journey keep out in deep water. On their return they hug the coast in shallow water and it is then that they are caught, often in millions.

Of the two modes of capture—drift net and seining—the latter was the only mode used at Newquay.

The seine, or stop-seine, is a fine-meshed heavy net some thousand feet long and seventy feet deep. It is weighted with leads along one edge and corked along the other, so that it is buoyed upright in the water. The seine net was carried in the seine-boat in the waist of which it formed a mound, stowed in such a manner that it could be readily shot by the men who were adept at the work from long practice.

Two other boats in attendance were the "volyer" (follower), which carried the tuck-seine, and the "lurker," a smaller boat carrying the master-seiner.

There were nine seines with their cellars, etc. The oldest was the "Spy," on Towan Head, just beyond the neck. Others were "The Fly" "The Good Intent," and "The Active," on the cliffs under the Beacon. The shelter and

UNITY CELLAR (Exterior)

A. A. G.

promenade occupy the site of the Active. The " Toby " was situated at the lower end of Tower Lane. " The Rose Cellars " were at the head of the road leading to the harbour. The houses of Trevose Place now stand on the site of this cellar. The " Unity " Cellars stood at the bottom of Gover Lane, where a shelter has been built, and the " Speculation " was under the cliff, where the Cosy Nook during the " season " is the scene of a very different activity.

Of much later date was the " Hope," built in Tower Lane. Its name still survives in Hope Terrace.

Each collection of seine boats, cellars, etc., was owned by a company and the master-seiner was the moving spirit. Of scarcely less importance was the Huer, who was one of the oldest and most experienced of the company's men.

On the edge of the cliff just under the Atlantic Hotel can be seen the Huer's House, still in a well-preserved state. When the fish were expected, the Huers of the various seines watched from the Huer's House for the shoals, the presence of which was indicated by flocks of gulls and patches of reddish tinge on the sea. When the shoals became evident below the Quies, each Huer with his megaphone-like trumpet, which was longer than a coach horn, shouted " Heva," " Heva." " The Cry is up," and " The Cry is up " would spread throughout the locality causing an excited but methodical haste, such as is never seen now-a-days.

As the shouts were echoed from cliff to cliff, from St. Columb Minor to Crantock, a frantic rush was made by all concerned, who left their immediate occupations, and rushed down to the quay to their particular seine boats, urged on by the cries of their respective huers.

Before the season opened, the various companies arranged which seines should take up certain stations in the bay. These positions were settled by casting lots, and the men knew exactly the stations to which they had to hurry when the cry went up.

When the shoal came within the area apportioned to any particular company, the seine was shot. The volyer kept

the end of the net taut while three men in the seine boat shot
the seine, the boat being rowed swiftly, yet gently, around
the shoal until all the net was in the sea.   Meanwhile, the
master seiner, with his eye on the movements of the fish,
gave directions to the rowers of the seine boat.   When the
net was shot, its two ends were warped towards each other.
the lurker taking his station at the opening to drive the fish
back if they should attempt to escape by the only aperture
available.   When the ends of the seine were in contact they

UNITY CELLAR (*Interior*).

were laced together and unless there were rocks or the water
was too deep the fish were safely secured.   If the water was too
deep so that the corks were not at the surface the net was
warped into shallower water in the Gazel, where it was
moored by grapnels (locally known as grapers) on every side.

Nothing further was done till the next tide, to give the
fish time to become quiet and accustomed to their imprison-
ment.   Then followed the next operation, known as tucking.

Tucking was carried out by another party of men (the
" regular seiners ") when the tide was low.   The tuck-net was
a smaller net, which was cast within the seine net to the side

of which it was drawn so that it contained a mass of fish. Then the fish were lifted from the net by means of a wicker basket, called a flasket. This had two handles and was manipulated by two men, who sat over the gunwale with one leg in the boat, and the other in the water. They dipped the flasket into the mass of fish, then lifted it up and after allowing it to drain, poured the fish into the boat.

Sometimes several million fish were enclosed in the seine and the process of tucking would occupy a week. After each tucking the seine was drawn in closer around the shoal, so that the enclosure became smaller day by day.

When the tucking was over the fish of the Spy, Fly, Active, and Good Intent, would be drawn up to the cellars from the boats, but the fish of the other seines were landed at the quays and taken in carts to the cellars.

The men carried the fish in " mauns," and " gurries," to the women who " bulked " them on the wooden floor under the lofts ; that is in the cloister-like area around the open centre of the quadrangular cellar.

Each woman started by laying on the floor a row of fish with their tails towards the wall. The fish were laid side by side and overlapped one another slightly. Between this row and the wall other fish were laid to cover the floor back to the wall. Then the salt, which was brought in small mauns, from the salt house by children, was spread evenly and thinly over the fish, and another layer of fish and salt added, and so on until the women had built up a solid wall of fish, possibly five feet high and two feet thick. At this stage the perpendicular face of the solid mass consisted of fish-heads pointing outwards.

Having built this wall of fish the women increased its width by putting a similar wall in front of it, and by adding to it in this way, if the catch was sufficiently large, practically the whole of the "cloisters" at the sides under the lofts were filled with fish " in bulk."

During this operation everything was streaming with sea water brought in with the fish. The women wore " pattens " on their feet, and hessian " towsers," or huge aprons tied tightly back to protect their clothes as much as possible, but notwithstanding this, the women were very wet at the end of each day. The cottages during the season were redolent of fishy odours while the clothes were being dried.

The fish stayed in bulk for about six weeks, during which time the oil drained from the bulk into the long drains beneath, which, from the inclination of the floor, led to a pit at the end of each cloister. These pits held perhaps a hogshead of oil and other fishy drainings.

As the salt dissolved, the men from time to time put more salt on the fish or threw salt against the wall of noses at the faces of the bulk.

Next came the breaking out of the bulk by experienced men and women. Alongside the face of the bulk was placed a " wriggle" on a " horse." The "horse" was a heavy frame-work on four legs. On the top of this was placed the wriggle, a circular wooden sieve with coarse wire mesh. By the side of this was placed a " gurry," a sort of box, the sides of which were prolonged to form a pair of handles at each end, so that two men could carry it. The men used a flat spade-like implement, to break out the fish, carefully taking out a small quantity at a time, from the top of the bulk, with as little injury to the fish as possible. These were placed in the " wriggles," which the women shook, so that the fish were freed from a considerable amount of salt. The fish were then turned into the gurries, which were carried by the men to two long wooden troughs, standing side by side at one end of the quadrangle where there was a drain. In this part were a well and a pump, from which the troughs were partly filled with water. The fish were thrown into the troughs and scrubbed down with stiff brooms to cleanse them. During this process the scum of filth and oil rose to the surface of the water and was removed and sold to soap boilers. The fish were taken from the first trough with long-handled gridiron-like scoops and thrown into clean water in the second trough. After being scrubbed the second time the fish were beautifully bright and shining, and were again put into the gurries and taken out under the penthouses around the outside of the cellar. The barrels were ready and the women waiting to pack them. The barrels were cylindrical and not bulged like ordinary barrels.

The women then carefully arranged the fish in the barrels. Each layer consisted of a circle of fish arranged radially with all the heads at the periphery against the sides of the barrel and the centre filled in with a " rose " of fish, tails alternating with heads.

In this way, layer by layer, the fish were packed to fill the barrel. Then on the top of the fish was placed a "buckler," which was a circular wooden cover made to slide in the barrel. The barrels stood in a row along the wall under the penthouse. At a higher level than the tops of the barrels, in the wall, was a row of square holes, in which were placed the ends of strong poles. Between the buckler and the pole was put a block of wood. Then a heavy stone, in which was an S-hook, was hung by a rope from the end of the pole. This lever system caused the fish to be pressed with so great a force that the buckler soon went down to " three-quarter hoop," while still more oily matter found its way to a drain beneath and so into the pit. After the fish had been pressed down the barrel was filled up again to the top, and again the same pressure was applied. In this way the barrel was filled with a solid mass of fish.

Next the heads were put on the barrels and fastened securely. The barrels were branded with the name of the cellar, and were then ready for the buyers.

When the price was settled the buyer picked out a barrel here and there. These had their heads removed and the bucklers replaced : then the barrel was inverted on the bucklers and the hoops cut, so that when the barrel was lifted the cylindrical mass of fish was left standing on the buckler.

The buyer took out a fish here and there to see that they were well-preserved, and if satisfactory a new barrel was put down over the fish and sealed up.

The barrels were shipped at the harbour for Mediterranean ports.

Next came the " troil," which always terminated the pilchard season. This was a feast provided for those connected with the cellars, each cellar having its own troil.

After the feast, which was given in the loft, games and dancing followed. These were kept up until the small hours of the morning, the music being provided by a fiddler ; and from my recollection the dances were folk dances, many of which have been revived of late years.

Chapter V

FARMING

N EWQUAY was the market centre for a considerable
farming district.

The headlands and adjacent sandy areas were sheep
runs, while on the deeper, richer soils further from the coast,
grain and roots were grown. In the light soils oats and
barley were the chief crops, while wheat was grown on the
richest soils.

Oxen were commonly used for tillage operations and even
as draught animals on the roads during the earlier half of the
19th Century. Between 1850 and 1860 I can remember seeing
ploughing with two yoke of oxen and a horse leading : and
I have distinct recollections of oxen at Treringey. The driver
who attended to them would sing some kind of refrain in time
with their rhythmic gait, calling each by its name and using
a long goad when necessary to accelerate their movements.
The goad was a pole, six or seven feet long with a point at the
end, and appeared to be a very effective instrument for the
purpose it was intended to serve.

At the same period a large number of women worked on
the farms. Reaping was done by women with reap-hooks,
and though scythes, and, still later, cutters and binders were
no doubt profitable, yet the primitive method of reaping
was a far more pleasing sight. A row of women in
their light dresses and sun bonnets, laying low the corn as they
passed like a wave over the field of ripe grain was a far more
satisfying picture of rural life than the modern methods which
have rightly made their toil unnecessary.

When the last sheaf was cut, the reaper held it up and
shouted, " I have 'en. I have 'en. I have 'en." The others
who stood around answered, " What have 'ee ? What have
'ee ? What have 'ee ?" and the reaper replied "Anek ! Anek !
Anek !" Then they all shouted " Hurray !" To " Cry the

neck" was quite a little function, and we made a point of
seeing it.

If the weather was settled, the corn was put up into
shocks, but if unfavourable conditions seemed likely to pre-
vail, the corn was built into round mows about eight feet
high. These were called " Harrish Mows," because they
stood on the stubble, which was known as " harrish." When
dry, the corn was carried to the " Mowey," where they were
stacked. After that came the harvest supper.

Sixty years ago threshing was usually done with a flail,
and the corn was winnowed out of doors on a breezy day, when
the winnowing sheet was spread. Women came and collected
chaff and carried it home. This chaff was called " doust."
The corn was sent to the various mills to be ground, the near-
est mill being situated at Rolly Point.

With the growth of the town, farming on the peninsula
has been restricted more and more, until now only the farms
of Tregunnel and Trethellan, and one or two market gardens,
remain.

CHAPTER VI

———

THE GANNEL

EXCEPT during the season when visitors are moving to and fro about the estuary, the Gannel is more or less deserted.

At other times a few tradesmen's carts splashing through the shallow stream which flows along the Newquay side of the sands, or the boats which ferry across those whose occupation makes it necessary to go to and fro, are the only evidences of active life.

To those who have lived near it, and who know all its varying moods, the Gannel has an attraction which no casual visitor can even faintly appreciate.

Probably the Gannel is seen at its best at high water during spring tides. This always occurs during the evening, and in calm sunny weather, the clear lake-like inlet reflecting from its surface the many-coloured low cliffs, meadows, and trees, makes a picture of peaceful beauty not often equalled. At such a time, when the tide has reached its highest and there is no stream to disconcert even the laziest or most incompetent of rowers, to pull quietly from one point to another with an ever-changing view, and a quietude which enables the slightest sound to be distinctly audible, makes it difficult to realise that just over the way is a wild coast beaten with the long Atlantic rollers.

But the Gannel at low water with its sandy surface varying in colour from place to place, and scored by its windstream glistening here and there in the sunlight, is far from unpleasing ; while during dull weather, when the rolling grey mists are continually blotting out headlands or disclosing them to the view, the Gannel cannot be considered to be commonplace.

During the last century the Gannel was a far more important estuary than it is at present. Its economic importance is now negligible, but formerly the work done on the Gannel was considerable.

Vessels came into the Gannel and were moored in the river just below the Fern Pit on the Crantock side facing the bottom of the road down from the village. To keep the stream on the East Pentire side of the bay a breakwater was built and the remains of it can still be seen. As the boats lay against the high sandy bank they were discharged and loaded. Coals were brought for Crantock and the mines near it, while the vessels also discharged cargo into barge which went to Trevemper, taking coals, manures, limestone, and earthenware.

Iron ore from the Perran mines was carried away, the ore being brought to Crantock in carts and dumped in two fields near the " Sailor's Well," which may still be seen on the left of the road going up to the village from the beach. I have seen as many as nine vessels in the Gannel at oue time. No vessels ever loaded or unloaded above the Fern Pit. During rough weather they were moored by the side of the small quay just above the point at the Fern Pit, until calm weather came enabling them to be hobbled out to sea.

Rings and hooks are still to be seen in the rocks on the West Pentire side of Crantock beach, and I have heard that formerly vessels were discharged and loaded on that side.

In Newquay Bay vessels were towed out by hobblers in boats, but from the Fern Pit the hobblers towed the boats with ropes, to keep them in the river, walking along the cliff until they had pulled the vessel as far as the cove near the point. Then the tow ropes were cast off and the vessel put out to sea.

Several men were regularly employed as bargemen. Boys were bound as apprentices for " barging," as for any other trade. The barges were loaded from the vessels and when the tide began to flow they were carried on the stream guided by the men on board up to Trevemper Bridge. The empty barges were brought down on the outgoing tide. Trevemper was then a seat of some activity and possessed large stores for many kinds of goods, manures, coals, earthenware, hardware, oils and colours, farming implements, etc.

In those days there were many more houses atTrevemper, and a chapel stood at the Cross on the road to Crantock.

The remains of a small quay may still be seen at Penpol Creek. On the end of the quay stood a small kiln to which barges brought limestone.

All the boats which would not be needed during the winter were brought round from Newquay harbour and moored in the Gannel against the bank in front of Tregunnel. These boats included all those connected with seining as well as pleasure yachts. Going round in the boats was a pleasure to which we looked forward and was one of the events of the year.

The ship-building yard stood just below Tregunnel. It was owned by Messrs. Clemens and employed quite a number of hands. I remember several vessels being built there— Glendorgal, Penpol, S.M.C., Tregunnel, William Martin, Edith, and Guiding Star.

Launching always taking place at high water on a spring tide, was an evening event, and there were always many people present to see it.

The boats were launched side on into the water from this yard, and, as they took the water, caused a huge wave to spread across the Gannel. Of course there was the usual " naming " ceremony, when a bottle of wine was broken against the bow as the vessel was leaving the stocks.

For fitting out, the vessels were usually towed round into Newquay harbour.

The houses recently built on the slope between Pentire Farm and the Fern Pit constitute the most noticeable change in the appearance of the Gannel.

In the shelter of the rocks which projected through the thin soil on this steep slope there grew narcissi, in striking contrast to the heather and sea pinks which coloured the Dennis further down.

Even in the Gannel in the old barging days there were exciting times.

One night when wind and tide were travelling in the same direction Henry and Robert House were running their barge to Trevemper early on tide. She was laden rather deeply and struck the point of the marsh just opposite Tregunnel House. She swung broadside on, and began to fill and soon sank. The two men clung to one oar and called for help. They had been in this perilous position struggling some time before their cries were heard. A young man came out from Tregunnel to have a look round before retiring for the night. He heard the cries, called his father who had one to bed, ran down and put off in their boat and rescued them.

Another day the barges were going down to the bar opposite the Fern Pit to load, on the out-going tide. The wind was blowing out of the Gannel very strongly and the tide running like a chain. Each barge carried when laden, from ten to fifteen tons, so were not easy to manage under such circumstances. When they touched the bar, one of the two men had to watch his opportunity and jump ashore with the rope to make it secure. This he did, but the barge swung round with such force that the painter broke, and man and barge were carried out of the Gannel. Nothing could be done there to reach the man, so one of the men from another barge ran off to Newquay, raised the alarm, and one of the gigs was soon manned and off to the rescue. It was a very exciting time as they were afraid the barge would drift out of sight before they could come up to her, and night was coming on. But, by bending to their task, they succeeded in reaching her when down off the Gull Rocks, and brought her back. What anxious hours that man must have spent before he sighted the gig coming to his rescue !

One summer evening a party of five from Tregunnel House went out in a boat, but off Penpol Point they were caught in a squall when tacking. Undortunately the rope attached to the sail was fastened. This of course ought not to have been done ; the rope should have been held in the hand

Bathing machines on Towan Beach.

A view towards the Promenade (now Narrowcliff), showing a boat being unloaded. The long, low building is the Speculation Fish Cellar. Note the absence of buildings on the Island.

The harbour, before the Atlantic Hotel (opened in 1892) had been built.

The harbour at the end of the nineteenth century.

The fishermen associated with Unity Cellar.

A bumper catch.

A practice launch on Lifeboat Day, which was usually held on August Bank Holiday.

Coastguard cottages that once stood in Fore Street.

Bank Street, looking towards Central Square.

so that it could be slipped free at any moment. The gust of wind filled the sail, the boat capsized and threw all the occupants into the water. Three out of the five were drowned. The bodies of the two ladies were seen floating and were recovered the same evening, but the body of Mr. Silas Martyn was not recovered until next day. It was a sad ending to what seemed to bid fair to be a bright and happy day.

CHAPTER VII

MINING

NEITHER the visitor nor the modern resident, who has not behind him a Newquay ancestry, ever realises that mining was a serious occupation on the peninsula at one time.

The sea and the harbour, as well as various relics of fishing and sea-faring life, render it tolerably easy to realise that once upon a time these occupations were two of the mainsprings of life in the town ; but the mines are not only well nigh forgotten, but there are now few remains to show that mining was carried on—even the mounds of refuse having been removed.

All the mines in and around Newquay were lead mines.

Near the bottom of Trethellan Hill a mine was started. The shaft was sunk, but when it became necessary to instal machinery, though some parts of it were brought to the mine and a boiler was put in, lack of funds caused working to cease, somewhere about 1860. Since then the engine house and other buildings have become more and more ruinous and very little now remains to mark the site. Water still runs from the " adit " in the low cliff at the bottom of the hill.

The Lehenver Mine was on what is now called Mount Wise, and the only buildings there at that time were connected with the mine—counting house, carpenter's shop, blacksmith's shop, and captain's house. When the mine was no longer worked these buildings were converted into cottages and so commenced Mount Wise as a residential quarter. The mound of mine-refuse known in Cornwall as a " burrow " was carried away to fill up the hollows in Lehenver Lane.

A little time after the mine closed, Mr. Robert Bunt opened a school in the counting house. He was a retired coast-guard, having served away from Newquay.

Young sailors, who wished to qualify for a captain's post, attended his classes to learn navigation. Bunt was undoubtedly a clever man but like many others of that genus never got on. It was at that time that Bunt gave the name Mount Wise to this, the highest part of Newquay.

The " adit " from the mine came out of the cliff about half way along the Town Beach. A wooden shute was raised suffidiently high for carts to come along and carry away the water in barrels for domestic purposes when water was low in the wells.

A water company was formed to supply the town, and a public demonstration took place at the opening in 1884. This water was brought from Quintral Downs to the reservoir on Mount Wise.

In 1889 a windmill was erected by Mr. James Pearce to pump water from the mine shaft to supply the houses on Mount Wise. Later it was bought by the water company, who deepened the shaft and replaced the windmill by a pumping engine.

The Fistral Mine on the low cliff was called North Wheal Providence. William Phillips, who worked the engine, was from the neighbourhood of Tywardreath. I mention this because the guide books of Newquay, among their very many errors made by writers who either knew nothing about the matter, or took no pains to verify their statements, say that the mine was an iron mine and was not worked. I also remember seeing the lead in little heaps on the " floors." A considerable amount of the " burrow " of this mine was used to fill in the shaft, but until quite recently a portion of the burrow still remained on the top of the cliff.

There was another mine between Tolcarne and the Narrow Cliff. It was known as Tolcarne Mine, and an " adit " was driven into it from the beach. The " burrows " of these mines have been used locally for the mending of roads.

On the Crantock side of the Gannel, between Penpol Point and the road leading from Crantock to the Beach, lead was smelted. The smelting house stood nearly at the top of the hill and from it ran two diverging trenches to the beach. These trenches are still evident. The lead ore came mainly from the Penhale district.

Silver was separated from this lead, and I have heard of a very large plate of silver being lodged in the Albion Inn at Crantock for the night before being sent on to London.

The smelter's name was John Steward. His cottage adjoined the smelting house. I have heard my mother say that in one of her walks to Crantock she had tea at the cottage with Mrs. Steward.

When it was found less expensive to take the ore away than to bring coal to the Gannel, it was shipped to Swansea for smelting. Then Mr. Steward with his wife and adopted daughter came to Newquay and lived in one of the cottages in Norman's Court. It was then that I came to know them.

The mines which supplied the Gannel vessels with iron, were a part of the Great Perran Lode, Gravel Hill, Mount, and Treamble. The Treamble iron lode was sixty feet wide. It had, parallel to it, a lead lode four feet wide. The iron was worked as an open quarry by the Cornwall Mineral Company.

It was a sad time for many families when East Wheal Rose Mine was flooded and all the men in the shaft were drowned. Two sisters, one with five young children and the other with three, lost their husbands in this catastrophe and were suddenly plunged into the deepest sorrow and poverty. There was no compensation or insurance money to assist them in the struggle that ensued. Many under such cirdumstances would have abandoned themselves to grief and despair. Not so these women. Realising that it was not a time to sit and nurse their grief they bravely rose and faced the future and worked long weary hours to maintain their children and fit and educate them for their future life.

CHAPTER VIII

———

SMUGGLERS AND SMUGGLING

I N 1800 there were only two coastguards at Newquay and two at Kelsey Common. The old house at Kelsey stood right on the cliff about midway between Polly Joke and Holywell. From the house they had an uninterrupted view of the coast for many miles extending from St. Ives to Trevose. Most of the watching was however done from the Revenue cutters at sea, the men being known as " cuttersmen." Notwithstanding the vigilance of these men when cruising up and down the coast, the smugglers often eluded them. Even if they were seen and it was known that a cargo of coutraband goods had been landed, by the time the Revenue officers had put off and come ashore in their small boats, all would be safely stored away in secret places, and the smugglers would be standing round in groups or gone back to work cloaking their satisfaction with an appearance of remarkable innocence, which anyone but an experienced Revenue man might mistake for utter simplicity !

We know little or nothing of the hardships endured by the men and their families before they took to smuggling ; but I will give one or two instances of impossible prices which had to be paid for common articles of food.

When my father was a boy some ninety years ago salt was sixpence a pound, so that if a poor man fed a pig, he would be obliged to sell one half of it to procure enough salt to cure the other half. Tea was twenty shillings a pound ; a prohibitive price for poor people to pay.

In addition to this economic incentive to smuggling there was the love of adventure which is inherent in every child born on the coasts of our island. So that, when all is considered, it is little wonder that smuggling was practised. It is rather surprising that smuggling was not even more extensively carried on.

As regards the actual arrangements we must remember
that there was a distinct understanding between the crew of
the ship bringing contraband and the men on shore who were
prepared to take the goods.   The latter were banded together
in a sort of secret society, and all had fictitious names.   I well
remember a few used in Newquay—Curlew, Robin, Chough,
Justice, Soldier, Gannet, Red. etc.   They imitated the notes of
the birds in calling each other at night time.   Then again there
were secret signals given on board the ships and suitable
answers returned if the coast was clear for landing the cargo.

A signal similar to a natural phenomenon was often used
to baffle the Revenue men :   thus will-o'-the-wisp played an
important part in these cargo running enterprises.

The men on shore knew all the beats of the coast guards,
and hence were certain where they would be at particular
times.   Thus if the cargo was to be landed in the Gazel, a time
would be chosen when the coast guards would be on the Crantock side perhaps meeting the Kelsey men at Treago.

Supposing the vessel was laden with tea and spirits, the
tea would be taken out first and carried into the cavern below
the cliff.   Then it would be drawn up into the tea hole.   Many
a time have I been down the path and I know something of the
danger he men ran to secure their cargo.   The casks of spirit
were small so that a man could easily carry one.   If it were
not safe to land the spirit then, the casks would be strung
together to a heavy chain and sunk beneath the waves.   From
certain marks on the cliffs they were easy to find when the
way was clear.

There was always a certain amount of ballast in the
bottom of the ship to keep her right in case of heavy weather
and with this she could run for some port near, get a cargo and
take it to a port where another cargo of contraband could be
obtained.

Sometimes a cargo would be run in on Crantock Beach
and stored in Piper's Hole.   When we were children it was
said that there was a passage from Piper's Hole to the smuggler's hole under the kitchen floor of the farm house at Treago.

The cavern is now almost blocked up with sand, but I remember when we could go a considerable distance into the hole.

I knew where several of the store places were and have been into some of them. Under the blue stone floor of old Stephen Hoare's kitchen there was a secret cellar. Another was under Richard Carne's kitchen : one could go down the stone steps which led out under the wall to the saw pit under his carpenter's shop. The wood was piled up on end and nothing was to be seen of the cellar or either of the entrances to it.

At Tregunnel, on the left-hand side of the lane going out from the farmyard there was a smuggler's hole behind the woodrick. I have been in that one many times. There was another near the back door. This was made into a duck house later. In the kitchen over the fireplace was a secret tea hole. Some of the small beams could be taken out and this exposed a secret chamber in the wall of the chimney. At Tolcarne there is still to be seen, in a quarry on the estate, near the viaduct, a smuggler's hole cut through the solid slate stone.

At the Albion Inn, Crantock, there was a large secret chamber under the kitchen floor. I have often knocked on the blue stone near the chimney and heard the hollow sound beneath.

From the road below Treago Farm where the cartroad leads down to the mill, one can see, by the side of the stream, a series of depressions in the bank where the sand has fallen in and filled the holes which at one time were used by smugglers for storing cargo.

Once, when the men who were removing cargo at Crantock found they were being watched, they hid it in the Belfry. The smugglers knew the revenue men were too superstitious to follow them into the churchyard, and thus escaped detection.

The definite plan was that as soon as the goods were landed they must be got to their destination as soon as possible. Men on horseback were sent off in all directions to make

arrangements as to time and place where they were to be met
on the road.

Of course funds had to be raised for those smuggling
affairs, and this was accomplished in much the same way that,
in earlier times, the Merchant Adventurers adopted. They
pooled sums of money and freighted ships to bring home
merchandise. The merchants ran the risk of pirates cap-

COAST-GUARD LOOK-OUT.

turing their ships and cargoes and so losing all they had ven-
tured.

The organisers of a smuggling venture were very similarly
placed. They had to risk capture by the Revenue Cutters
as the merchants had to chance loss from piracy. However
from a personal stand point the main difference was that the one
venture was recognised and even commended by the State,
while the other was discouraged by various punishments.

The smuggling venturers were generally farmers or professional men, who pooled both their gains and their risks. The men who watched for, and landed the cargo, and undertook its distribution, were paid wages. Their risk was greater even than their masters' because if they were taken they suffered loss of liberty and in some cases loss of life also.

It is true that the risks they ran were very great, but the punishment, if they were caught, would be still greater.

One man at Crantock was suspected of knowing where a cargo was stored. He was taken out to the cutter in the Bay and questioned, but pretended all through to be silly, and, as opportunity offered, asked the most ridiculous questions about the boat and the men. I have heard him tell the yarn : how he asked the Captain if the little black things up there were the crows' nests !—(meaning the pulley blocks used for hoisting the sails). The Captain became so disgusted with him that he told the men to take the fool ashore and see that they brought someone next time who knew something !

On another occasion at Crantock a man was held a prisoner for a day and a night in his own kitchen ; which, by the way, was a part of the old College, that had been converted into a cottage, and where, in the long ago, Henry VII. had been educated, This man had a large family and was extremely poor, so they thought it possible to tempt him with money. Consequently they turned out a bag full of guineas and told him that it should be his if he would tell them where the cargo was stored. He persisted in saying he did not know : nor did he, as it had been sent to its destination the night before. His daughter told me afterwards how she longed for her father to tell so that they might have the money, which would have meant so much to them. But he was faithful to his comrades and refused to give any information. His daughter asked him after why he didn't tell. " Ah Mary," said he, " Thee'st hang the men for the sake of the money."

To show how poor they were and what the money would have done for them, Mary told me they never had anything but bread made from barley. The only time they had white flour was when their mother at Christmas bought some for the Christmas pudding.

Can we imagine what Christmas must have meant to such children ?

And yet these men are often considered as criminals for trying to get common necessaries at a cheaper rate for their families !

We can scarcely estimate the difficultues experienced in those far-off days in getting the goods away after they had been landed.   Many of the roads were so narrow that two coaches could not pass each other.   In many places there were semi-circular refuges into which one conveyance could be drawn while the other passed on.   Until 1760 there was a lack of coach connection with the west part of Cornwall.   The turnpike extended no further than Falmouth and round Penzance the roads were merely bridle tracks.

As evidence of this bygone mode of personal conveyance from town to town there are still to be seen many " upping blocks," especially at farms in this neighbourhood.   These were provided to help riders to mount and dismount from saddle and pillion.

Trevemper bridge is a good specimen of what bridges were like in the old pack-horse days with its V-shaped recesses for sheltering pedestrians and low parapets to allow the packs to swing clear.   Most of the smuggled goods were carried on horseback.

The custom was to range six horses in line, five tied head to tail, and then load them with the packs.   Two such lines with two drivers conveyed the goods to inland towns.   Many stories could be told of smugglers and their doings, but one more must suffice.

A vessel stood in the offing out from Crantock Bay. There was no Revenue cutter in sight, so, seaward all looked propitious ; but, alas ! the coastguards had changed their night and the Newquay men were meeting the Kelsey men at Treago. They met, exchanged the watchword, and the Newquay men would return by way of Crantock and would see the strange light off in the Bay. It was a time when " men must work," and arrangements made sharply and quickly. The coastguards must not come back through Crantock, and the cargo must be got ashore. How was it to be accomplished ?

Four of the men went to Treago iron gate with strong ropes, hid until the two coastguards were coming through, captured them,and tied them to the gate securely,back to back, one on each side. There they were left until morning when someone passing by liberated them. Thus the cargo was landed and the coastguards none the wiser !

CHAPTER IX

THE WRECK OF THE SAMARITAN

A N East Indian Trader, a brig of Liverpool, 248 tons N.M.,
named the *Samaritan*, was caught in a storm off Bedruthan on Oct. 22nd, 1846. The brig was bound to Odessa
and Constantinople.

She was driven on shore and dashed on a large rock near
" Queen Bess." becoming a total wreck. Since that date
the rock has been known as the Samaritan. Only two out of
a crew of twelve survived this terrible tragedy.

She was laden with all kinds of merchandise, exquisite
Indian silks and satins, lace, muslin, print, house-linen and
other material, as well as provisions of various kinds.

After the wreck there was hardly a house in the whole
countryside but could show large quantities of all kinds of
material. The farm houses could have silk cushions on the
benches even in their living rooms. By the next summer
there was scarcely a young woman but came out in beautiful
figured muslin dresses. Every bed quilt had its new patchwork cover and even to-day one can still be shown, in old
coverlets, pieces from the Samaritan cargo.

Very soon after the vessel struck it was seen that the
cargo would be washed out of her and carried in all directions
on the raging waves to be stranded eventually in caverns,
crevices of rocks, sanded in deep pools or on open beaches.
Those who have watched such wrecks know how impossible
it would be to salvage such a scattered, water-logged freight.
The Customs officers, though present, would be powerless
to do anything to safeguard a cargo under such conditions.
This wreck has been cited in books as an opportunity when
the smuggling propensities of the inhabitants along the coast
were let loose and indulged in. I believe much of the smuggling that was done in olden times was prompted as much by

the love of adventure as by the love of gain. In this particular wreck, had it not been for the sharp-eyed, energetic people, very little of the valuable cargo would ever have been found. It was they who walked the beaches hour after hour at low tides looking for signs in the sand, for portions of the cargo. Then a bit of bright-coloured material at the bottom of some deep pool would be an incentive to commence digging operations. Heavy material, such as some of the bales, would be sunk two or three feet beneath the sand, and it was no easy natter to reclaim it. To my thinking they deserved all they got after carrying for miles such material heavily weighted with sand and saturated with water. To the women and girls of that day this kind of excitement would appeal just as a bargain sale does to women of the present day. It may be interesting to follow a party of six young people on one of these excursions after wealth. They left Newquay, walked to Trevelga Height, and went down the face of the cliff at Hedge End.

Going down this almost proved a tragedy to one of the party. The foothold was partially broken away and, as they tried to go round the Hedge End they were suspended over the cliff with just their hands holding on to the stones in the hedge above them. One of the party failed, in swinging round, to catch the step on the other side of the hedge, and so hung suspended by her fingers. It was an awful moment for the whole party as they were all powerless to render assistance.

Fortunately there were others coming up from the beach on the other side of the hedge. Seeing the state of affairs one of the party caught hold of the swinging foot and placed it in the step and so saved what otherwise would have been a sad ending to their days' pleasure. When this party reached Bedruthan they searched among the rocks and were successful in each obtaining a load sufficient to carry back. The tide had receded far enough to ensure a dry passage through the calm. All this journey, work, and excitement justified a rest, so, sitting on the shelving rocks opposite Glendorgal, they compared their spoils. Coming towards them across

Porth beach at the same time was Mr. Llewellyn,the custom-house officer, and one of the coastguards.   They evidently intended crossing the river opposite to where the others were sitting.   What was to be done ?   Fortunately the dresses in those days had full skirts ; and by dint of spreading them to their utmost capacity they could cover their treasures.   The river was deep at the time so Llewellyn hesitated to venture through.   One of the young fellows of the party had his boots off and he offered to carry Llewellyn across.   Llewellyn than thanked him and said he should have plenty of wading to do before his return, so might as well begin.   So saying he took off his boots and stockings and waded over.   Then the party wasted no more time resting but picked up their parcels and made for home, going by way of Tolcarne, Trenance, and Tregunnel.   One of the party lived at Tregunnel.   They set to ; washed out what sand and salt water they could, and spread the material on some wood in the back of the old cart house, and went their several ways.

A piece of duck was among the material, and some of it was made into a pair of trousers for one of the big boys of the family.   This material was evidently intended to be worn in a hot, dry climate, and not for humid England.   The funny thing about it was that every time it rained the trousers stretched instead of shrinking !   The poor boy told me that pair of trousers was the terror of his life.   He knew that as soon as it rained his trousers would grow.   Hem after hem was turned up, but still at every shower the stretching went on.   When he saw any indication of a coming shower he crept in anywhere for shelter and watched.   He hadn't the pleasure out of what the *Samaritan* brought him, as did some of the house wives along the coast who were known to say—

"   The Good Samaritan came ashore,
To feed the rich and clothe the poor."

CHAPTER X

THE LIFEBOAT

THE hazards of a seafaring life have always called forth the best in the human character. Not only does it require physical courage to endure the hardships, but moral courage is also needed to enable the sailor to put up with the discomforts and the monotony of his calling.

But it is when danger comes—when the sea takes on the aspect of a deadly enemy to the mariner, that we see the unselfish side of the seafaring nature.

There was certainly something heroic and praiseworthy when our men, in the old days, voluntarily watched the coasts and, without an incentive from the outside world or any promise of remuneration, went forth in boats, not specially built for the purpose, to save those in danger. The only suitable boats available were the long narrow gigs, which are still used in rowing matches and regattas. These boats possessed only one of the characteristics of the modern lifeboat—that of rapid motion—but the men's one idea was to save life and this they did and earned the gratitude of those they rescued, as well as the respect of the general community.

At last however came the lifeboat specially designed for the purpose it was intended to serve. Great was the excitement in the town and many were the speculations among the youthful inhabitants as to the shape, size and capabilities of this wonderful new boat.

At that time there was not a family but had relatives actually engaged in a seafaring life, so the enthusiasm displayed was of a mutual as well as of a personal character.

We watched Georgie Burt's six great horses go out of the town one morning in 1860 to fetch home the wonderful treasure, and the talk all day was about the boat and the probable time of her arrival. In the evening all who could walk, trooped out as far as Narrowcliff. In those days this was considered a long distance,as there were no houses beyond the foot of Marky's Hill.

As it was dark we could only listen for the sound of the wheels ; but soon the word was passed along—" She's coming !" The thrill caused in all hearts as each one echoed the words, still lives in the memory. The horses were stopped, we crowded round ; we cheered ; we touched her ; and with feelings almost akin to reverence we felt we were welcoming a true friend. Then the signal was given for starting and we formed in procession and marched into the town to the lifeboat house.

A life-boat house had already been built, a little beyond the coastguard houses in Fore Street.

It is now used as a butcher's shop but the date can still be seen on the gable end.

When the boat had been drawn to the boat house there came the excitement of backing her into the house and in the dim light of the lanterns she seemed a huge thing to be put into such a narrow entrance, but Georgie had a way of his own in talking to his horses, and they certainly understood his language when he shouted " Bauke, hosses, I say bauke !!" and after various backings she was eventually lodged in her house.

On the evening of the christening and launching she was taken down into the harbour (there was no jetty there then) and got ready for the ceremony. By mutual consent the honour of christening this, our first lifeboat, was accorded to Mrs. Willie Michell. The young squire looked very pleased as he led his young wife down the old walk into Quay Hill from the Fort Grounds and stood hat in hand during the whole ceremony. A hymn was sung, prayer offered and then Mrs. Michell stepped forward to the boat and said " I name you Joshua,and when you go forth on the mighty waters, may you like Joshua of old and as your name implies, be the saviour of men."

Then came the first launching.

We watched the men as they put on their cork jackets for the first time and took their seats ; after which she floated off from her carriage. This caused great excitement, but there was still more to follow. She was taken across the harbour to the steps of the North Pier and all the moveable tackle was taken out. Long ropes were passed under her and made secure and the other ends of the ropes were handed up to the men on the pier. These set to work with a will and soon she was upset and we had the pleasure of seeing all the crew floundering about in the water. The boat righted herself beautifully and several of the men scrambled back into her again but the others continued floating about. I heard one, I think it was Bill Burt, call up to the men on the pier and say '' I know nothing about swimming—but it's all right. I find I can't sink with this jacket on.''

Everyone seemed fully satisfied with this her first testing, and felt that with such an efficient boat a new era in rescue work had dawned on Newquay, and that there would be far less to dread now than formerly when the winter gales came.

The rocket apparatus had been in use since 1844 and the men had done good service with it in rescuing many crews from stranded vessels.

Chapter XI

———

THE REGATTA

NOT only did the early inhabitants of Newquay indulge in such recreation as skittle games and hurling, but Regattas were held annually in the bay.

In those days our men would have scorned the idea of holding a regatta in the Gannel ! That would have required no dash or daring and would have been far too tame to waste on it the energies of the young life of Newquay.

The first regatta I have any account of took place in 1815. Newquay was noted for illuminations and decorations on public holidays ; and I never remember the Regattas in my young days without having before me recollections of the gay decorations.

The day before the regatta trees were planted in the streets and arches made and decorated with flags and flowers. There was always a band, and, if the town had no band at the time, one was hired from St. Columb, St. Dennis, or Truro.

One regatta which I distinctly remember took place on Midsummer Day, 1857. Hundreds of people flocked into the town from early morning, coming from all parts of the county. They came in every conceivable conveyance, from a donkey chaise to a four-in-hand. Then there was the coming of the gigs. They came usually from Padstow, Fowey, and Charlestown, to row against the Newquay crews. These boats were brought by land on wheels and taken down into the harbour. Then there was a feeling that the fun and excitement had commenced.

Booths were erected on the Beacon between the entrance road and the Huer's House. Six or eight booths, according to the number who had taken out a special licence for the day. The Committee booth stood in the centre in full view of the race course marked out in the Bay. For the children there were a large number of standings where all sorts of things were sold—fruit, sweets and toys, from a ginger-bread man to a monkey on a stick. It would be no exaggeration to say that there would be thousands in the town by midday to join in the festivities.

The yacht racing began at 10 o'clock in the morning, the starting of the races being done on the Beacon from the Committee Booth. Of course all of us had our favourite boats and we watched the race with keen interest.

The gig race excited most interest because of the visiting boats and there were so many outsiders to prevent there being an overwhelming number to support any particular gig. We were jealous for the honour of our Newquay crews and could not bear to think of the First Prize leaving the town. Selfish, wasn't it ? Well, you see, people nowaday say we lived in such isolation then, and, that being the case, what else could be expected of us ?

One year we had a Ladies' Gig Race, but I had better not say much about it because everyone is supposed to know that it is not the province of a number of ladies to pull together !

Another year the chief feature was a race for men over sixty years of age. There were three entries.

In 1889 there were two regattas—one in the Bay and one in the Gannel. The boat house at the Fern Pit was used as Committee Boat and starting point. It was found that the reach up to Penpol Point was too narrow to allow scope for the fantastic rowing of ladies, so Penpol Point was decided upon as the more convenient place for starting. I have rowed in regattas both in the Bay and in the Gannel and so know something of the keen enjoyment the competitors take in the sport ; and even if it does seem somewhat egotistical, I may say that I feel some satisfaction in never having won less than a Second Prize !

The one race of the day which never failed to create amusement was the punt and gig race, which generally meant a ducking for the one who tried to board the other boat. After the racing came the sports on shore : donkey racing, hurdle racing, etc., but perhaps most fun was caused by the climbing of the greasy pole for the leg of mutton which was securely fastened to the spike on the top of the pole.

The grease was laid on with no niggardly hand, so that it required courage, patience, and not a little pluck to reach the prize.

The finish of the day's sport was the dance through the town to the strains of the band. Those who were taking part lined up in front of the Red Lion Hotel, and nothing but the Flora Dance could be accepted as a suitable end to the day's festivities.

Chapter XII

HONOR POTTER (Mrs. Scoboryo)

THERE was one particular shop window in Newquay sixty years ago which never lost its charm for the youthful part of the population. How we watched the various movements that were taking place therein ! With what new interest did we view any and every added treasure to that window ! Even the re-arrangement of the goods already there arrested our attention and aroused our curiosity ! No : it was not a grand plate-glass window. It was simply a twelve-paned kitchen window situated in the gable end of a two-roomed cottage. The bottom ledge of this window outside was about eight or ten inches from the raised foot-path, and served as a seat from which we could make our imaginary selections. The cottage stood end on to the street on a very small part of what is now Jenkins' China Stores. The door was in the side of the house facing the Central Square. The door proper was always open but there was a hatch or half-door with a little bolt on the top ledge, and this was generally barred. I remember how on tip-toe I used to reach up and slip it back when I wanted to enter. Every minute detail of this kitchen was familiar. A general air of quiet and comfort reigned in that little room. There never seemed to be the confusion of turning-out days and yet it was always clean in appearance, with its evenly sanded floor and well-dusted chairs.

Hanging on the wall opposite the door was an old " head and hinge " clock with its face, on which was a floral design. By its side hung the portrait of some ancient dame, whose eyes seemed to follow you no matter in what part of the room you stood. To the left of the door, the settle with a high round back shut off the chimney corner from inquisitive eyes, and made it look as if it must be a real haven for the privileged few who might be invited to rest within for a while.

The dresser stood between the clock and the window : it contained the usual three shelves. The topmost shelf held the glass of the house, the second contained the quaint old china, while on the lowest was the earthen ware. How bright and shining it all looked !

In the corner between the window and the door were the stairs, the door of which was so arranged that the two bottom steps protruded and looked as if they were overflowing and would not be kept behind the scenes.

There was a bench in the window and, above it, two narrow shelves across the panes of glass. Before the bench was a table fitting close to it so that it looked like a continuation of the same.

The half doorway and the little window were the only means of admitting light to the kitchen ; hence it is easy to understand that the room must have looked dark and dingy to a child. Yet dark though it looked, it did not prevent me from entering whenever the opportunity offered, and, to my judgment, it never offered too frequently. Why ? It was not because of the attraction of Honor Potter who presided over the establishment. If anything we stood rather in awe of her : but perhaps if I describe her and her dress you will the better understand.

She was a grave little woman of few words and rarely if ever was she seen to smile. She moved, too, with quiet even step, and looked as if she could keep her own counsel and attend to her own business. With her the fashions seldom changed. I always remember her wearing a close-fitting goffered cap and a large white muslin neckerchief, the corners of which were tucked beneath the band of a print apron. The apron almost covered her short black frock.

Neither was the great attraction the window proper in which were displayed bottles containing all kinds of goodies— long sticks of liquorice, acid-drops, almond comfits, nuts, peppermints, also ginger-bread men, with their bits of gilt paper on their foreheads.

The chief and only attraction for some of us was a large tin box which stood at the left-hand corner of the little table and looked very like a cash-box. This box was the pivot round which all our hopes and wishes revolved.

From our vantage ground outside the window we recognised the sound made when the lid was raised. There, with eyes centred on the one object of interest, we watched the counting out of five or ten of Honor's bulls' eyes. They were the much-loved and coveted sweets of the whole country side—brown, shiny, and dry—such beauties !—with no stickiness as there was with those which we in our ambition tried to concoct. Of the making of them—the how, when, or where—we knew nothing, nor could we have said, had we been asked, whether Honor kept the shop, or the shop kept Honor. All we knew was that the box, the bulls' eyes, and Honor were always there wooing us to enter, and, whenever we were fortunate enough to possess the essential, we needed no other invitation.

Honor was a proud, reserved woman and I suppose it was her reserve that rather awed us as children. We never seemed to make any headway with her in matters of conversation. As soon as we paid her for the bulls' eyes our business was ended and we felt there was nothing left to do but beat a hasty retreat.

Honor's maiden name was Glanville. She married, early in life, Joseph Scoboryo. They had six children—all girls. They seemed to inherit the independent spirit of their mother. Only one of them settled in Newquay : that was Nancy, who married Stephen Hoar. Mrs. Snell settled in Plymouth, Mrs. Tilley in London, Mrs. George went to Australia, Mrs. Wickett to Boscastle, and Amy went to America. Their family history could be traced back four hundred years from the parish books. The Scoboryo's had been a wealthy family, but why the name of Potter was given them I do not know unless it was in connection with the smuggling fraternity.

I have said, in another chapter, that each member of a band of smugglers took the nickname of the band—Robins, Curlews, Reds, etc.—and that in some cases, doubtless, in course of time, these nicknames became surnames. Possibly " Potter " may have had the same origin.

CHAPTER XIII

EDUCATION. MY SCHOOL LIFE

UNDER this heading it is difficult to know how to classify the scrappy instruction we received in those far-off days.

Education was then in an embryo state : the teaching was an attempt to instil into our brains a conglomeration of ideas which we might or might not assimilate and from which we might obtain some little measure of benefit.   In the light of what we now consider educational advantages, we possessed none, and yet without their aid we managed to compete somehow with others and hold our own in the commercial world.

Accustomed to life on a wild coast, we were not daunted by trifles, and so " picked up " information which served us as a substitute for education.

We possessed no Elementary, Higher Grade, Secondary, Grammar or Technical Schools, and consequently our educational advantages were very limited and may appear to some altogether too ridiculous to be classed as such.

The inhabitants being so few there was no scope for separate schools eighty years ago : consequently those who wished to have their children educated sent them to the villages that were more central.   For example, my mother walked out to St. Columb Porth and attended a Mrs. Hammott's school.   My father and the young Johns' walked from Tregunnel to Trencreek to a Boys' School there.

In 1840 Mr. Stephens opened what was then considered a first class Boys' School at St. Columb Minor and the boys walked there from all the villages around.

There were no endowments for schools of any kind in the neighbourhood, so the fees paid by the scholars must have been sufficient for the upkeep of the school and teacher's salary.

Perhaps if I state my earliest recollections of school life, I shall give a general idea as to the early education of most of the children in the town at the time. I with several other little girls and boys attended a "Dame's School" next door to Honor Potter's. The mistress, or teacher, was Mrs. Harriett Sleeman. The kitchen served as schoolroom and she divided her attentions to us with her ordinary household duties. While these duties were in progress, our thoughts generally were taken up with what was going on outside. There were three rows of moderately high forms placed opposite the door and I very well remember the difficulty I had to keep my balance, for if my feet touched the floor I could not reach the form, so I was kept alternating between seat and floor, and when, in desperation, I did manage to plant myself on the form, I lost my equilibrium with the result that the back of my head succeeded in finding the floor more easily than my feet had done, much to the amusement of the other children. At this school I was taught to rèad, write, and knit. The knitting was a terror to me : the stitches would persist in going wrong, and, try as I would, I could not remember that it was the last stitch in the row that I must knit and the first I must slip. How the needles would assert themselves and do the wrong thing in spite of all my infantile patience !

Dame School number two had a more soothing influence on my nerves. It was situated in the row of houses opposite the old lifeboat house. The teacher was Mrs. Peggy Clemens. Being older, my legs were a better match for the forms than in the previous school. There was the usual reading, writing and arithmetic to be contended with. Varied occupation was a term unknown in the school curriculum of those days; yet we were given employment that might very well have been classified under this heading. It consisted in the stuffing of a cushion and for this purpose we had to pick out " tiflings " or " ravellings " from odd pieces of material and with them fill the cushion.

One great source of amusement at this school was the frequent visits to the door of Will Clemens' talking jackdaw.

When we saw the way clear we fed it and this induced it to come all the more frequently. At such times Mrs. Clemens would go out and lecture the bird and try to drive it away, but Jack seemed rather to enjoy the altercation and would answer back with impunity—in which respect he had the advantage of us.

As the population increased, good schools were started and I soon found myself one of Miss Jane Sleeman's pupils at what is now known as Shirley Cottage. She kept house for her father, Captain Robert Sleeman (generally addressed as Cap'n Bob). The room on the left hand side of the door was the subscription Reading Room. Our schoolroom was the kitchen and was situated on the right hand side of the front door. Although supposed to be at our lessons I am afraid we generally managed to see who passed in and out of the Reading Room each day. We entered the school from the field at the back of the house, down an easy flight of steps into the garden. There was a deep rough trench round the back of the house, and I have a lively recollection of scrambling down into it one morning more briskly than was comfortable.

At the Fort opposite the school young Master Willie Michell had, among other pets, a tame raven. I hadn't much faith in its tameness and may as well confess, was really afraid of it. The most provoking part was that it would come into the school garden without even being encouraged, as the jackdaw was, in the other school.

For me the climax came when, just as I closed the garden gate and started to run down the little slope before coming to the steps, I was confronted with the raven ! It did not croak " Evermore," but simply looked and I looked too, and went to the bottom of the trench at top speed. I scrambled out and entered school with greater alacrity than I had ever done before. There were several complaints lodged against the raven, and shortly after it was sent away.

One of our chief enjoyments while attending this school, was playing in the large garden which extended from the house to the two cottages beyond. In this garden Evans and Sons' Monumental Works now stand.

A very high hedge separated the garden from the Quay Road. On the garden side of this hedge were six sycamore trees which still remain and remind some of us of the many times we climbed their trunks with the aid of the friendly hedge, and sat among the branches watching the passers by.

It was a good garden for fruit : such large black currants and red and yellow gooseberries ! We watched the bushes most assiduously when the fruit was ripening—to keep off the birds !

This school was a great advance on the other two from an educational point, and much more was required of us. We saw a good deal of household management and work, and ought, at least, to have had a fair insight into the practical side of Domestic Economy. We worked well at our lessons generally, but, alas ! there came a day when six of us played truant ! The temptation was great but the uncomfortable consciousness of doing wrong was far greater. One of the girls told us that lots of Barcelona nuts were being washed in on Fistral Beach and suggested our going out that afternoon to look for them. That was my first and last venture at " minching " as truanting was called. Any good intentions we thought we had went to the winds, and so must the nuts have done, for we could not find any, although we walked the beach the whole afternoon looking for them.

Some little time before this, the Misses Jewel with their father Mr. George Jewel, surgeon, came to reside at Harbour Terrace, from Trevemper Bridge where he had had a practice. Up to this time there was no doctor in Newquay and with the exception of Doctor Jewel there was none nearer than Newlyn East or St. Columb Major, but Newquay then, as now, was a healthy place and the absence of a resident doctor did not cause us much anxiety.

The Jewels rented two of the houses in Harbour Terrace and opened a large boarding school. When we left Miss Sleemans' we went to the Misses Jewel as day pupils. At that time they had about twenty yearly boarders. After school the boarders went off in procession on their long walks

accompanied by one or more of the Misses Jewel. There
were five sisters and they shared the work, both of teaching
in the two schoolrooms and in managing the two houses.
In the room overlooking the harbour and bay Miss Sarah and
Miss Kate taught the boarders and Miss Nanny taught the
day pupils in a room looking out on the street. Miss Susan
was the housekeeper and Miss Fanny looked after her father
and his patients. They were a busy hive of workers and I
think could have held their own even against our modern

GOVER LANE.

teachers. They had one mode of punishment which I have
never known practised in any other school and it was very
effective. If any of the pupils needed a lecture or were dis-
obedient, they were sent into the room of the other teacher,
and there had to state, before the pupils, the reason why they
were sent, and had to bring back a faithful report as to what
the other teacher thought of their behaviour. It was a

terrible ordeal and needed a great amount of courage to state exactly what was said. I remember being sent in once, and ever after tried to avoid a repetition of the experience.

They were good women, true and dignified, and commanded the loving respect of all who knew them.

After I left home when I went back for my holidays I was often invited to tea with them in their private room. During one of those visits the conversation turned on accomplishments, and I expressed my sorrow in having had so few advantages, when Miss Fanny replied in her quiet way, "Don't trouble about accomplishments : good common sense is what is required to be successful, and you have a good share of it." That little stimulating sentence has often been a great help, especially when I have felt inclined to doubt my ability and think it not equal to the responsibilities resting on me, or the duties I had to perform.

There was no good boys' school in Newquay until about 1860. Then one of the ushers from the St. Austell Grammar School came and rented the upper part of the Malt House and named it the Alma Place Academy. Boys came from Crantock, Cubert, Lower St. Columb, and all the farms in the neighbourhood. The number who came was a strong proof that such a school was needed.

At the request of some of the parents that their daughters might share in the advantages the teacher consented to take a limited number for arithmetic in the afternoons.

I, with six or seven other girls, readily embraced the opportunity for continuing our studies under the new methods, which I found were a great help to me in after years.

There was just one thing which happened while I was there which showed that boys, even in those days, could be chivalrous. We were allowed out for recreation at 3 o'clock for about ten minutes. The cannon pit was near and its sand banks were a temptation. One day we remained out longer than the allotted time, and when we realised what we had done we all rushed down into the yard to find the teacher standing on the topmost step with one hand behind his back.

John Crocker, one of the boys, passed the word along, " Look out girls ! He has the cane. Pack in close to the first lot of boys as they go up the steps, and we'll all follow and make a rush for the door. Then we shall get the stripe and you may escape." We did as he said and, thanks to his quick thought and sympathetic interest, avoided the punishment.

It can be seen that what we lacked were suitable rooms, text-books, and apparatus. As regards teachers and pupils, they did not appear to be lacking in capacity even when tested by modern standards.

In July, 1868, the permanent population of the town was 1100, and for some time it was felt there was a want of a more extended education. Efforts were made to establish a Parochial School and Dr. Treffry gave the site. Plans were drawn up for the erection of a school and a school-house, with a brick-tiled roof. Brick tiles were unusual in Newquay. The estimated cost was £400, and to raise this amount a two-days' bazaar was held in Killacourt field, lent by Dr. Boyle. The ladies presiding at the stalls were Mrs. B. Williams, Carnanton, Lady Tylden, Mrs. W. Michell, Mrs. Treffry, Miss E. James, Misses Tippett and Mrs. Treneer. The following gentlemen gave their assistance : Mr. Carus Wilson, Rev. N. F. Chudleigh, and R. Mildren. The receipts of the first day exceeded £100. A very successful concert was given in the evening in the Town Hall or Assembly Room in Commercial Square.

Later the foundation stone was laid by Mrs. Treffry in the presence of a large number of people.

In June, 1870, the Bishop of Exeter opened the school, and it was ready for the reception of scholars in July, when a first-class certificated mistress was appointed. The school was entirely under the control of the Rev. N. F. Chudleigh and his curate, until February 1875 when the first School Board was formed to manage the Newquay and St. Columb Minor Schools.

Twelve gentlemen were nominated for the five seats, but seven withdrew to avoid a contest. Those elected were Messrs. Boyle (Newquay), Richard Cardell (Trebilsue), Cotton (Trenance), Nicholls (Penrose), and Stephens (Gustivean).

At their first meeting Mr. R. Cardell was elected chairman and Dr. Boyle vice-chairman. Mr. James Pearce was elected clerk. The meetings were held alternately each month at Newquay and St. Columb Minor.

CHAPTER XIV

EARLY POSTAL ARRANGEMENTS

I HAVE heard my father and mother say that from 1820 to 1830 there were no means of communicating with the outside world by letter, unless specially paid messengers were sent with them to St. Columb Major or Truro to post.

One wonders now how the lovers managed to convey their sentiments one to the other when unable to meet ! It must have been a severe test to any of the sailors who had made love to girls in distant ports. Possibly they practised " thought reading," and in this way wafted on the wings of the wind the wireless messages they wished to communicate all unknown to those by whom they were surrounded !

The first regular system of letter sending was exceedingly primitive. A certain Mrs. Brown of St. Columb was enterprising and far-seeing enough to know that even the people of Newquay could not live by fish alone and so combined the business of butcher with that of letter carrier. She came once a week in her pony cart and performed the double duty of bringing the supply of animal food and the letters. On her return journey she took back with her the letters she had collected during the day while disposing of her meat. There is something rather refreshing in the thought of the people's simple trust in her honesty. It was not then deemed necessary to take an oath before a magistrate in order to ensure the safety of the letters.

This mode of letter carrying continued until August 14th, 1837 ; when the postal officials thought Newquay was of sufficient importance to have an office, and appointed Miss Jane Marshall postmistress. She was then 25 years of age and was paid the extravagant salary of three guineas a year. Her father was Custom House Officer at the time and had

The Red Lion Hotel, decorated for the same Royal visit.

Central Square in 1909, decorated for the visit of the Prince of Wales. The Central Hotel had no less than four different names during its existence.

The Town Porter, with a row of 'jingles' (ponies and traps), outside the railway station.

The engine turntable by Cliff Road.

1905: an excursion arriving at the railway station.

Narrowcliff, once known as the Promenade, in the 1920s.

A coal boat at Porth Beach.

1932: the Prince of Wales watches as marshland is dug to form Trenance Lake. The men digging were unemployed volunteers, who received only dole money and a pasty for lunch each day.

Trevemper Mill, destroyed by fire in 1963 and demolished in 1964, is shown on a map dated 1693. The last recorded miller was Henry Salmon, 1914.

built an office in their front garden on the corner of Beachfield Avenue.

There was of course no Beachfield Avenue then ; just
three cottages with fields behind. This office Miss Marshall
shared with her father and eventually it became recognised
as the Post Office.

At the same time Thomas Rawlings was appointed
postman for taking letters to and from Newquay and St.
Columb Major. He accomplished the journey on foot three
times a week but either the walking proved too much or the
remuneration too little as we find him resigning the post on
August 1st, 1838. Even then August was a busy month
and, as letter carrying must go on, Thomas Bullock (known
later as Tom Post) was selected for the duty.

All goes well for a while, but on January 10th, 1842,
when the Act for the penny postage was passed, the business
so increased that it was necessary to give much more time
to the work and so we find Miss Marshall venturesome enough
to apply for an increase of salary ! This being granted she
was now the happy recipient of £5 a year.

The next special favour shown was to the postman who
was granted the use of a donkey and cart for the journey
and for carting the parcels round the town when distributing
the letters. The people also shared in this improvement
as a *daily* delivery was then established.

The postman left for St. Columb about 9 o'clock in
the morning with the despatch. and returned at 3 o'clock
in the afternoon bringing with him the letters which he
then delivered. I remember we generally looked out for him
when coming from school.

Sending letters from Newquay was an expensive luxury
before the introduction of the cheaper rates. It may be of
interest to the young folks if I give a few specimens, taken
from one of the old official books, of the rates of postage
from St. Columb to various places in England.

Each letter to and from St. Columb and Newquay was
4d. extra to the charges mentioned in the official list—

London 1/-, Darlington 1/2, Cardiff 11d., Bristol 10d., Kingsbridge 9d., Ilfracombe 8d.,

In course of time Miss Marshall married Mr. Samuel Salmon the butcher and they settled in a house in Central Square where Mr. T. Jewell's shop now stands. The room on the right hand side of the door was used as a post office.

At that time the converting of an ordinary room into a post office simply meant removing a small pane of glass from the bottom row, and inserting a small black board into the aperture with a six-inch slit across under which were painted in white the words " Letter Box " and the whole was complete.

Through the kindness of Mrs. Hoyle, Mr. and Mrs. Salmon's daughter, I have a copy of a quaint petition they sent to the Post Master General asking for an increase to their stipend. The signatures attached are those of the most influential people in the neighbourhood at the time.

To the Right Honourable the Post Master General.

The Petition of Samuel Salmon who is Post Master at Newquay (No. 1) from St. Columb, Cornwall.

Humbly sheweth that your petitioner's wife Jane Marshall was appointed Post Mistress at Newquay in August, 1837, at a salary of £3 3s. 0d. per annum and in 1842 your Lordship was pleased to augment her salary to £5 0s. 0d. per annum. Your Petitioner now most humbly begs to state that since the last mentioned time the population of Newquay is much more numerous and the increase of letters both forward and delivered being so greatly increased that it requires the whole attention of himself or his wife to this duty.

Your Petitioner therefore most humbly hopes your Lordship will be pleased to condescend and take the same into consideration and augment the salary for such duty in addition to the present as your Lordship may seem meet. And your petitioner, as in duty bound, will ever pray—

We the undersigned most fully corroborate the above statement.

Dated Newquay, June 28th, 1849.

Gordon W. F. Gregor, The Tower.
Jos. Thos. Treffry, Place House, Fowey.
F. Rodd, Glendorgal.
N. F. Chudleigh, Incumbent of St. Columb Minor.
John Cardell, Yeoman, Newquay.
George Jewel, Surgeon   ,,
Henry Andrew   ,,   ,,
William Stephens, Yeoman, Porth.
William Mitchell, Barrister, The Fort, Newquay.
William Martyn, Merchant, Porth.
S. E. Martyn, Merchant, Trevemper Bridge.
John Martyn, L.M.
William Benny, Yeoman,
W. B. Bennett, Incumbent of Crantock.
Richard Johns, Yeoman, Crantock.

The above petition was acceded to and Mrs. Salmon continued in office for nearly twenty-three years, resigning on April 14th, 1860, when Mr. J. Reynolds was appointed postmaster and a part of his shop was used as the office. This was opposite the Central Hotel.

On Feb. 24th, 1872, another change was made and Mr. W. R. White became postmaster. A few years later he built the house now occupied by Mr. F. Whitehouse, on an approved official plan, so that it could be used exclusively for postal affairs. Consequently this was considered the first real post office.

I must add my meed of praise to the memory of Mrs. Salmon, the pioneer of postal work in Newquay. Having known her personally for fifty years I can truly say she was a woman of sterling worth, courteous alike to rich and poor in her public capacity, and her quiet gentle manner never failed to command respect. She was a clever needlewoman too and found time amid her multifarious duties to execute some fine hand-made lace, as well as some beautiful silk patchwork. She died in the early part of 1899 in her eighty-eighth year and we all felt that her death was the severing of a valued link with the past.

CHAPTER XV

EARLY VISITORS TO NEWQUAY

THE present generation has never known a time when a more or less extended holiday in summer was not the rule.

It may be that modern life tends to be more exhausting to nervous energy, and that a more minute division of labour brings with it more monotony in individual occupations.

Modern life may also have brought in its train a more highly strung nervous organisation.

Be that as it may, it is an undoubted fact that we never knew anything about one's nerves being " on edge " ; and being " fed up " was not a condition common amongst us.

Even those who cannot get a few weeks holiday a year, have the picture houses, and football or cricket matches, as well as other means of obtaining relief from the mental activity connected with their employment.

In the old days we lived a simpler life. Hours of labour were long, but work was of a more placid character, and there was no haste, neither was the last ounce of energy extracted from the human machine.

Sunday seemed a sufficient provision for rest, and religious exercises a means of recreation giving the mind a set of ideas to act upon, totally different from those connected with the daily toil.

Occasionally there came the markets, the fairs, the troils, and, dare I say it, the revivals, providing diversions the more exciting because of their comparative rarity. But, when all is said, I think it must be admitted that our lines fell in quieter if not in less pleasant places than those of the present generation.

Even in those early times there were a few people who, by reason of their occupations as well as because of their means, had time for extended holidays, and who found a congenial change in sequestering themselves in a spot where coast and sea are unrivalled in grandeur and beauty, and where the ever-changing moods of the sea prevent a lover of nature ever feeling monotony in his surroundings.

In those days, when visitors were the exception, the natives, either from curiosity, or from wishing to show a friendly spirit, watched with deep interest their coming and going and, I had better confess, tried to find out all they could about them without appearing to be inquisitive.

Every little incident was treasured up so that it could be retailed during winter evenings or at special gatherings.

One of the first noted visitors I remember was Mr. J. T. Tregellas. It is true he came only from St. Agnes, but being a lecturer and author of many amusing Cornish Tales, we were always ready to welcome him, especially as he was thoroughly conversant with the Cornish rural population, and was equally capable of reproducing their peculiarities.

I heard the late Mrs. Nicholas Hocking, of Primrose House, relate that, when he was staying with them, he did, unknown by her, what she had never seen before.

One morning at the breakfast table, after he had eaten an egg, he turned the shell upside down in the egg cup and passed it to her when she came into the room late, and requested that she would share the remaining eggs with him. She took it and commenced cracking it, only to discover the deception, much to the amusement of the company.

Tregellas was so full of humour and of such a genial disposition that one could readily understand his setting such an innocent trap for her. We were sorry to hear of his death which took place in Wales in 1863. It was his wish to be buried under a particular yew-tree in a little church-yard on the banks of the Dee.

About 1860 the poet, B. W. Procter, better known as Barry Cornwall, was a visitor here. He was frequently seen driving a pair of cream ponies in a low four - wheel carriage. In his walks he would stop the fishermen if they were about and converse freely with them. I have wondered if it were from these visits to Newquay that he used the pen name of " Barry Cornwall," as " Barry " was a common name here at that time. After the death of his eldest daughter, " Adelaide Anne" the poetess, in 1864, he never came again, possibly because of his great age.

He stayed at " The Retreat " and should the street door be open, he could be seen of an evening walking on the verandah overlooking the harbour. From this open doorway when passing, I have often enjoyed a glimpse of the bay, as the rays of the setting sun illuminated the upper cliffs. The effect of light and shade was very pleasing.

Dr. E. B. Pusey was a frequent visitor after the great controversy and his suspension for three years from his pulpit. He would spend several months here at a time and showed great interest in any public affairs that might be happening during his stay.

He was in the habit of coming here from 1853 to 1871, so that we came to look on him as an old friend.

He visited at various places. One year he stayed at Trenance, another at Porth, and another at West Pentire.

While he was at Porth he had the steps on the left side of the " Calm " levelled, so that it became safer to walk through the little gorge between Porth Island and the mainland for those who wished to visit the caverns and beaches beyond.

Another year while he stayed at West Pentire he caused the road to the well to be improved and the steps below to be cut wider so that the beach became much more accessible.

He was here in March, 1863, when the Prince of Wales (King Edward VII.) was married, and helped to make the time memorable. It was a general holiday and the children met at their different Sunday Schools, marched to the Central Square, and united in singing several songs, after which tea was provided for them in the street. The old folks over 60 years of age also had tea in the Life-boat House. At night the town was illuminated and Dr. Pusey who was then staying at Prospect House, in addition to having all the windows illuminated, had, in the doorway facing the sea, a full size illuminated representation of the Prince in Academic Robes. It was a splendid idea and well calculated to fix both the date and the event on the children's memory.

In the summer of 1871 he was again at Newquay and often could be met of an evening walking on the Headland and seemed to enjoy watching the setting sun and the varying cloud reflections on the sea.

Dr. Boyle once related to me an amusing story in connection with Dr. Pusey and himself. Dr. Boyle was returning from Trenance where he had been visiting a patient and had gathered some snowdrops in Mrs. House's orchard. Wishing to keep them from fading, and to have his hands free, he put them in the crown of his silk hat. Just as he was crossing the railway at the foot of Marky's Hill he met Dr. Pusey and raised his hat to salute when, alas ! down showered the snowdrops around him. Dr. Pusey came to the rescue and helped to gather up the scattered treasures. Dr. Boyle fancied from his looks that Pusey enjoyed the incident very much more than he did ; and it was a rather unusual sight to see a D.D. and a Surgeon together stooping to pick up snowdrops from a railway !

One of our early noted visitors was Dr. Alford, Dean of Canterbury. He was often to be seen sauntering on the various beaches, or sketching or finding out little bits of the history of local affairs. Writing in 1868 in " Good Words " he gave a scathing description of Humphrey's Folly—the Eyrie in Watergate Bay built by a local squire as a habitation for his mistress.

" Passing over the smooth sand we reached the steps cut in the rock to the " Eyry," a former pleasure house, and now abandoned in consequence of the undermining of the foundation by the disintegration of the front of the cliff. Nothing is more dreary and forlorn than the abandoned modern building. With ancient ruins it is widely different. But these ruins of sham prompt no feeling but disgust— staring mullioned windows adapted for modern sashes, round would-be towers capped with the inevitable battle- ments about six to a tower, and all the rest in keeping. What is such a ruin but a monument of the flunkeyism which has well nigh eaten out our national manliness ? On there- fore with little more than a passing look, up the steep path by which the lord of the '" Eyry " used to turn his back on his " folly " and re-seek the top of the cliffs."

I think this description of his ramble to Bedruthan Steps is equally good.—" I took care to carry home a photograph beside my two hurried sketches that I might not be supposed to have been romancing. There she stands done in stone, crown, profile, ruff, hoop and all, a weird, uncanny, gi- gantesque figure, unquestionable to the dullest fancy."

I think for a concise description of Queen Bess nothing could rival this.

It was the custom of the Gregors of Trewarthenick to spend two or three months of each year at the Tower, which was their seaside residence. The children of the town quite looked forward to the coming of the family each year. The word went round—" The Gregors are coming "—and to our small and limited ideas it was almost equal to the cry in Lucknow—" The Campbells are coming "! You may well ask why the day and hour of their arrival was enquired for with childish eagerness. All this excitement centred round a large *white* caravan-like conveyance. This was the Gregors' bathing machine and the first ever seen in Newquay. It generally arrived the day before the family—a kind of harbinger ! Compared with the modern pill-box bathing machines now used, it seemed a huge affair. When the family was in residence the Tower flag was hoisted at sunrise each day.

The bathing machine, drawn by a pair of horses, was taken down to the Town Beach (then called Under-Cliff by the natives) at about 10 o'clock each morning. As there were generally friends visiting one or more of the four young ladies, the machine was none too large to accommodate the whole party, who walked down across the fields and common to the beach. Much to our regret all this took place while we were in school, but as I attended Miss Sleeman's School at Shirley Cottage I had the satisfaction of catching a passing glimpse of the machine each day on its way to the beach.

Mrs. Gregor was evidently the leading spirit of the family. She was a keen, clear-sighted, sympathetic lady, always trying to alleviate and minister to the wants of others.

She established a dispensary at Mrs. Carne's, where poor people could come and consult her at certain hours, and if medicine was needed she would supply it. This was a great consideration at a time when there was only one Doctor in the neighbourhood. During the winter months Mrs. Carne was left in charge to give out to the people what they required from the dispensary. One could not fail to admire Mrs. Gregor's noble nature. She was a welcome visitor in every home.

With all her generosity she never pauperised, as the folfowing will show.

When tea was sixteen shillings a pound—a price she knew far beyond the reach of poor families—to obviate this difficulty, so that they might enjoy the refreshing beverage she bought in large quantities and sold at reduced rates just the small amounts the people required. Over one of the doors at Trewarthenick could be seen this interesting notice— " Loveday Sarah Gregor, licensed to sell tea."

Were I a descendant of hers I should consider the memory of that one act the richest legacy she could bestow. Her intellectual gifts too were used for the benefit of others. When educational advantages were only within the reach of the few she would give her time, and spare no expense in answering letters or giving advice in legal matters. Her volumes of M.SS. are still kept as the treasured possessions of the family.

At the decease of G. W. T. Gregor, Esq., the Tower became the property of his son-in-law, Sir Paul Molesworth, who enlarged it and erected for the use of the family a Roman Catholic Chapel.

CHAPTER XVI

———

DOCTOR HUTTON

ABOUT the year 1857 the Rev. C. H. Hutton, D.D., formerly rector of Great Houghton, came, not as a transient visitor, but to settle in our midst and to make Newquay his home. He took Beaucliffe House, now known as Towan House, and brought with him his valet, his housekeeper, and Mary, the cook. The servants were all elderly and gave one the impression of being very loyal and faithful to their master.

The Doctor himself was about sixty-three years of age when he came and was a bustling, energetic, noble-looking, though rather stout old gentleman. He had unfortunately a mercurial temper, yet was always ready to apologise when he knew he was in the wrong. He was kindly and brim full of sympathy when he heard of needy cases requiring assistance or pecuniary help. He was not only anxious for the bodily health and comfort of the poor, but for their intellectual and moral culture also. When he came to reside in the town there was no free school where the children of the poor could receive even the most elementary form of education, but he soon altered this by renting the inner drying loft of the dilapidated old malthouse which formerly stood opposite Primrose House in Gover Lane. He had a bell fixed on the roof and started a free day school with my aunt installed as mistress of it. As the number of the scholars increased I was elevated to the dignity of youthful monitress. The Doctor visited the school regularly from 9-30 to 10-30 a.m. and gave the Scripture lesson. I remember how I used to enjoy that hour : he had such a pleasant manner when teaching, and would be greatly amused at some of the answers given to his questions. We all tried to answer, but the motive for so doing may not now be considered of the purest, as we knew there was always a packet of sweets to be produced at the end of the lesson and those who had answered best would be specially favoured. All went smoothly for some time, but one morning Tom, who was paid 12s. a year for ringing the bell,was five minutes late. Alas ! for the Mistress and Tom ! We soon found out that the quicksilver had risen with amazing rapidity that morning, as the old gentleman bustled into the school earlier than usual and demanded an explanation. My aunt tried to excuse the poor boy, but that wasn't right—it only showed she encouraged him—and if such a thing happened again, he would dismiss them both. We all thought it looked serious, but I think he must have believed in not letting the sun go down upon his wrath, for during the afternoon he came again and hoped Mrs. Solomon would forgive him. He felt he must apologise before the whole school as he had been so rude to her, and he hoped she would try and forget what he had said. As time went on we got used to those occasional breezes and they soon lost somewhat of their charm. Apart from these mercurial outbursts he was the soul of goodness. His deep sympathy with others in trial was never more fully displayed than in December,1861, when the sad news reached us that the Prince Consort had died. That morning he came, hat in hand, tears streaming down his face, and announced to all the school that one of the best and most beloved men that ever lived had passed away. Turning to my Aunt he said " If it had been possible, Mrs. S., rather than such a calamity should have befallen our beloved Queen and the nation, I would willingly have given my life, if by so doing his could have been spared."

Much more might be written respecting Doctor Hutton and the school, but I have said enough to show what a true benefactor he was to the children. The annual treat was always a great success. It was held in the field which is now known as Ennor's mead. What grand times they were ! But I don't think any of the children entered into the fun with more heartiness than the Doctor himself. He generally managed to have some young friends visiting him at the time, and they were deputed to take part either in suggesting and carry-, ing out games or in looking after the comforts of the invited parents.

We never realised how much he had been to us until death claimed him on February 12th, 1862, at the age of 68 years.

Then came the funeral day when we shared a common sorrow and mourned a common loss. It may have been childish grief but, oh ! how real it seemed to all of us as we were formed up on each side of the coffin of our dear friend. It was then that we could think of all his unselfish kindness, and tender thoughtfulness. It might truly be said of him—

" He brought thoughts of heaven into the hearts of men."

CHAPTER XVII

COLONEL MICHELL

THE life of Colonel Michell was so interwoven with everything calculated to benefit the inhabitants of the town
that it would be impossible to describe any improvements
which were made without mentioning his untiring energy and
his practical devotion.

William Edwards Michell was the only son of William
Michell, Esq., Barrister and Vice Warden of the Stannary
Court, and was born at Newham, Truro, in 1840. Shortly before his birth his father purchased the Fort from Humphrey
Williams, Esq., of Carnanton, and the family soon after took
up their residence there. In this way from his earliest childhood " Master Willie," as he was then called, was associated
with the life of Newquay.

As a child he was regularly to be seen in the company of
his mother or his aunt Edwards, when they took their drives
round the neighbourhood, and as he grew up he became a
familiar figure in the town.

I remember very well when he brought his little galvanic
battery, the first I had seen, into old " Cousin " James Tre-
bilcock's, and how delighted he was when we showed courage
enough to hold the handles for a shock.

He knew nothing of fear. It was no unusual thing to see
him, as we often did from our schoolroom at Shirley Cottage
walking on the high wall which surrounds the Fort garden
with as much ease and confidence as if he were in the street
below. He was a splendid specimen of boyhood, tall and
thin with all the grace and ease of limb which belong to it, and
with an indefinable charm not easy to forget.

The recreative side of his character seemed to have been
directed so as to combine mental training with physical pleasure. This is clearly shown by the two forms of recreation he

was the means of providing for the young people. They were
those which required both brain and physical endurance.

In 1857 he organised the first Regatta which I remember,
and encouraged the men who were competing to put forth
their best efforts for the reputation of the town. He took
very little interest personally in yachting or fishing ; not that
he had a distaste for the sea, as his morning dip off the rocks
at the Headland throughout the year proved, but he excelled
as a pedestrian and an equestrian. He made a point of having
a six-mile walk every day, and he was an exceedingly good
horseman, his military bearing making him a fine figure in the
hunting field.

His parents sympathised in all he did in the interests of
the young people, and his father in 1858 rented " The Old
Step Malt House," in Gover Lane and provided instruments
and paid an instructor so that his son might form what became, in after years, the Town Band. There were fifteen
young men chosen who were known to possess some musical
ability. They met twice a week for instruction and practice
and no expense was spared so that they might be efficiently
trained to become proficient players. Mr. Franklin, of Truro,
was the instructor, and came and gave them two evenings a
week.

Perhaps it will be of interest to some to know the names
of those fifteen pioneers who helped to enliven the dreary even-
ings. The bandsmen were : Mr. Willie with his silver cornet,
John James, Thomas Pappin, Jude Hubber, Pascoe Rickard,
Andrew Rickard, Nickolas House, William Rodda, Thomas
Carne, Thomas Clemens, James Hicks, William Cook, and three
Osbornes—William, who played the baritone, Francis the
cornet, and John, who was drunmer.

I remember when they played their first selections in the
Central Square and how the young folk stood round them,
and not only listened, but inspected the men, their instruments, and their new dark caps with the letter " N " worked
in red silk over the peak.

On Nov. 13th, 1860, Mr. Michell married Miss Charlotte
Maria, daughter of Philip P. Williams, Esq., of Stoke House,

Worcestershire. She, like her husband, manifested a keen interest in the public life of the town and readily supported him in all his public engagements. Soon after they were married she performed a very important ceremony—that of christening our first Lifeboat. This was succeeded by the naming of a vessel launched from the Gannel shipbuilding yard, the opening of bazaars, presiding at stalls, and I also remember on one occasion she presented silver medals from the Royal Humane Society to three gentlemen for rescuing two ladies from drowning when they were cut off on the outer rocks at Fistral.

In 1860 he was selected as the first chairman of the Newquay branch of the Lifeboat Society, and when the slip at the Headland was first used he was still holding the same position and was on board when the lifeboat took her first plunge.

He was an officer in the Royal Cornwall Artillery (Militia).

The first Cottage Garden and Horticultural Society was formed in 1867 and he was elected its President.

At the first show the band which owed its existence to his efforts, provided the musical programme. He was an earnest and liberal supporter of the society for many years.

The adoption of the Local Government Act and the formation of the Local Board in 1868 were mainly due to his exertions and he was unanimously chosen the first chairman, a position he held for many years.

Through his representation in 1870 the Board of Trade sent telegraphic warnings of storms to Newquay. These he made public by having a staff erected in the " Fort " grounds overlooking the harbour, where, as a warning to sailors, the drum was hoisted. This thoughtful act was greatly appreciated by the sailing community.

Local History and also Astronomy claimed his attention. In 1872 he gave two lectures in the National Schoolroom. one on the ancient history of Crantock and the other on Salt Cove, which included a good description of the view to be obtained seaward from the interior of the cavern and the exquisite colouring of the rocks.

He took a deep interest in Astronomy and wrote numerous letters to the local papers respecting the Planetary System for the benefit of juvenile amateur astronomers and in June 1874 received an acknowledgment of his work in this science by being elected a Fellow of the Royal Astronomical Society. In December of the same year he took his seat on the magisterial bench at St. Columb.

When the separate Burial Board for Newquay was formed in January, 1875, he became its chairman. In November of the same year the masonic fraternity residing in Newquay and neighbourhood were constituted and he was the first W.M. of the Lodge.

In thus enumerating the public offices he held I have attempted to show that Colonel Michell performed a very great deal of work for the public good ; and his amiability of manner enabled him to deal with many controversial ques-, tions without the asperities often associated with meetings of a public nature.

He knew nothing of bigotry, and whenever he could in any way help either of the places of worship, he was ready to do so ; not only speaking at meetings connected with the Church but often attending services at the Wesleyan and United Methodist Chapels.

In 1892 it became known that an operation was necessary, and he went to Woolwieh in the early summer for the purpose. But the doctors decided that nothing could be done to save his life. When the sad news of his death reached the town there was no one but who felt that a life of usefulness had been lost to the town and that a familiar figure would be greatly missed in so many ways.

An unfinished letter to his wife showed that his last thoughts were of his loved ones at Newquay. One can imagine Tennyson's language to be his—

" And may there be no sadness of farewell
When I embark."

CHAPTER XVIII

——

PLACES OF WORSHIP

N O early history of Newquay would be complete without an account being given of the introduction of the various religious sects, and the building of the different places of worship.

The first place of worship built in Newquay was the Ebenezer Baptist Chapel which was erected in 1822. Long before the chapel was built the Particular or Strict Baptists formed themselves into a community and met for worship in the old malthouse opposite Primrose House. They had a regular Sunday supply of preachers from Plymouth, Torquay, and Truro. In 1856 the Rev. John Bath took charge of the church, and continued to minister there for over twenty years.

The names on the lease for the land were: James Hicks, Henwood, farmer, Richard Kneebone, John Tippet and William Carrivick and the lease was granted for 5,000 years.

The first chapel was crowned with a thatched roof, but, several years after, this was removed and a slate roof put on. The slate was quarried from the cliffs on the Newquay side of Glendorgal Point, and Thomas Osborne was the mason who slated the roof.

There was one characteristic common to the first three buildings erected as places of worship: all had roofs which were four square, culminating either in a point or a very short ridge. This arrangement presented as small a surface as possible to any prevailing wind. The wisdom and forethought of this was evident when we consider how little protection there was for any houses built in open spaces so near the edge of the cliff and how insecure the slating would be with only one small wooden peg, about an inch long inserted in the slate to hang it on the rafter. In more recent times the slates are secured by means of long nails.

The worshippers at Ebenezer were Strict and Particular, or Calvinistic Baptists. The first members of the congregation were the Hicks (Richard, James, Johnson, and Henry), the Kneebones (Richard, George and their sister), Mr. and Mrs. Nicholas White, Mr. and Mrs. Bellingham, Mr. and Mrs. Thomas Pearce, Mr. and Mrs. John Solomon, Ellerys, Teagues, Pappins, Bunts, Hockins, Prouts, Moyses, and Mr. and Mrs. Tregidgo. When the accommodation became inadequate it was decided to build another chapel. The old building was taken down and a larger chapel erected on the same site. The new chapel seated 200. Mary Moyses was the first to be baptized by immersion in the baptistry of the new chapel in 1875. Previous to the erection of this building and baptistry, those who joined the church were baptized either in the harbour or on the beach. Some of the older members were rather opposed to having a baptistry—they considered it to be not strictly scriptural.

Since the present chapel was erected, a schoolroom with minister's vestry over it, has been added.

The old Methodist Chapel was built in 1833 at a cost of £170. From an old account book in the possession of Mr. Cotton Jenkin I find that the tradesmen were paid 2s. a day and the labourers 1s. 6d. each. The material was brought from Truro in carts. There were three divisions of seats with two aisles: the central division consisted entirely of high pews. The front halves of the side divisions also consisted of pews while the rear halves were made up of forms. There were twenty-four numbered pews and the sittings were let at 9d. per quarter. The forms were free.

In Mr. Jenkin's book are inserted the names of all those who took sittings, and I found my mother's name among them, she having taken her sitting in 1836. Later, following her mother's persuasion, she became a member of the Baptists.

The congregation soon increased to such an extent that in 1849 a gallery was added. At the same time a bell was hung in a little belfry on the top of the roof. This was the first bell ever used in Newquay for calling people to worship.

The conduct of the Wesleyan Conference from 1844 to 1848 resulted in a division of the church into Wesleyan Methodists, and Free, or Reform Methodists, the latter severing themselves from Conference. A division was also caused among the Methodists of Newquay. The majority sided with Conference, but the minority, for some reason or other, retained control of the chapel so that it was the majority, that is those, who sided with Conference, who left the chapel, the remaining worshippers calling themselves " Reform " Methodists.

These divisions led to very bitter feelings and the disputes were often conducted in a manner ill suited to the ideals of Christianity.

An old member of the congregation told me that when the final appeal was made by a local preacher, Mr. W. Cook, who was preaching his last sermon in the chapel, the following incident occurred.

Mr. Cook pleaded with the remaining " reform " members to reconsider their decision and come with the majority into the conference. The climax came when Cook said, " Remember, we go out from this church and take with us the cream leaving just the skimmed milk !" This ill-natured remark was too much for an old member, Mrs. Peggy Matthews who stood up in her place and looking not too pleasantly at Cook said, " 'Tis a lie Cooky and you know it " and with that she marched out of the chapel.

It is the custom to take a cynical view of these wranglings, but the very violence of these differences proves that the religious life of the people was a very real thing.

The going out of the Wesleyans in 1852 made a considerable difference to the numbers in the congregation ; but the remaining few were not crushed. With undaunted determination they succeeded in building up a strong cause.

The Wesleyan Methodist Chapel was built in 1852. It had seating accommodation for 450, and was the first place of worship in the town built in the Gothic style. It was always spoken of as Conference Chapel. I had cause to remember the building of it. Child-like I ran up over what I thought to be a dry heap of mortar, when, alas ! for my brown cloth boots, with patent toes, I sank deep into it, with the result that the boots turned red and were spoiled.

The opening of the Chapel was a grand day. After the Dedication Service, there was a tea and a bazaar held in the Town Hall. Large numbers of people came into the town, and the whole proceedings were considered a great success. Nearly all the principal farmers in the neighbourhood took sittings ; the Cardells, Treneers, Martyns of Trevemper Bridge, Roberts of Treninick, Martyns of Tregunnel, Sleemans of Tolcarne.

Those in the town who took an active part in the management, and were the principal movers in the matter, were the Tredwens of Eothen, Olwers, Reynolds, Carnes, Ennors, William Carrivick, Vivians, Hoopers, Willian Cook and Francis Hawkey were both Local Prachers. All these attended as families, not, as is often the case to-day, parents attending one place, and the children going somewhere else. Little Maria Hooper, as a child of eight, played the organ, and her father took a keen interset in the singing of the choir.

Billy Bray, the Cornish revivalist, during one of his visits to Crantock, came one Sunday morning to the service at which Mr. Francis Hawkey was the appointed preacher. Mr. Hooper, seeing Billy Bray in the back seat, mentioned this to Mr. Hawkey, who, at the close of the service, announced that Billy Bray would take the evening service. Billy's answer to this was : " Praise the Lord !" He dined with the Hoopers at Bothwicks House and at night preached to a crowded congregation.

The first quarterly meeting held in the town was on June 26th, 1889, and it was with difficulty that people could pass the Central Square owing to the number of vehicles there which had brought visitors to the meetings.

Of the new Wesleyan Chapel nothing need be said, as it remains a monument to the indefatigable energy of the Wesleyan community.

Meanwhile the " Reform" Methodists had been building up their congregation again, but once more they were fated to undergo division.

In 1857 the " Methodist Association" and the "Reform Methodists" united and formed themselves into a new sect —the United Free Methodists (the United Methodist Free Church). The Methodist Association had been founded in consequence of the expulsion of Dr. S. Warren from the Methodist body by the Conference because of the part he had taken in the dispute about the establishment of the Wesleyan Theological Institution.

These changes naturally affected the Reform Methodists at Newquay. An increasing number of them evinced a growing desire to fall into line with the new Church management. The result was that in 1865 another division occurred and the United Methodist Free Church was built near the bottom of Marky's Hill. A flight of steps leading up to the chapel caused it to be known as " Steps Chapel," while what was perhaps an even commoner appellation, " Spite and Envy" long bore testimony to the bitternesss with which the second flock separated off from the Reform Methodists. In later years when it became inadequate it was sold and the new chapel built in Beachfield Avenue.

I wonder sometimes, in looking back over all the vicissitudes the Reform Church had passed through, if some of the older member were inclined to say " All these things are against us"; while others among them of a more hopeful disposition might have answered with St. Paul, " It has turned out for the furtherance of the Gospel." After all the varied experiences that had arisen, another element of organisation seemed to dominate the church life.

Some influential congregationalists had settled in the town and neighbourhood and made their spiritual home in this old church. Among them was Mr. Richard Tangye, of Glendorgal.

Mr. John Cotton, a native farmer of Trenance, had frequently conducted the services and, altogether, was such an important pillar of the church that it was commonly known as John Cotton's Chapel. He continued to take the services there until the Rev. Hillier was appointed resident minister. The congregation increased so that in 1888 it was found necessary to build a new Congregational chapel.

JOHN COTTON'S CHAPEL.

The site was chosen and Mrs. MacArthur laid the foundastone stone on May 21st, 1888 and the chapel was opened on August 16th following with seating accommodation for 250. The old chapel was afterwards known as the Congregational Lecture Hall. It was used for lectures and Sunday school work until the new Hall. was built in Marky's Hill. Soon after this the old hall was sold and is now used as a carpenter's shop.

Thus we see that the spiritual forebears of those who now meet in the Wesleyan Church, the United Free Methodist Church, and the Congregational Church, were those earnest but somewhat difficult people who worshipped in the old chapel close to the line crossing Crantock Street.

The Bible Christian Chapel was built in 1851 in the Deer Park.

When the foundation stone was laid the Rev. William Allington stood on it and preached from the text, " All flesh is grass." The original lease was dated February 20th, 1851 and the names on the deed were those of William Rodda and Nicholas Lewarne of Porth, Richard Cardell, C. S. Martyn, Nicholas Hocking, John Clemens, Thomas Bullock and Robert Rawle. The first two mentioned on the deed were Local Preachers and were the moving spirits in having the chapel built. Before the chapel was erected they met in William Rodda's dwelling house. The Bible Christians were quite a distinct body from the other Methodists in Newquay. In the early days we always spoke of the chapel as the " Bryanite's Chapel." The name owed its origin to a Local Preacher in Cornwall named O'Bryan, he having separated from the Wesleyan Methodists in 1815. They differed from the other Methodists in allowing a larger proportion of the lay element in the management of the church, and they also trained women to become ministers. I remember Mr. and Mrs. Tregaskis preaching in the Bible Christian Chapel when I was a girl. They had their own method of conducting the service, each taking part in the same service. They were known throughout the community as " Father and Mother Tregaskis." They always drove to their appointments in their own conveyance, from their home Salt Water Mills St. Issey, so were not chargeable to the society for travelling expenses.

Billy Bray preached in the old chapel during one of his visits to Newquay.

I am indebted to Mr. J. Bassett Williams, of St. Columb Minor—a Bible Christian Local Preacher for verifying my notes. In 1889 a revival broke out during the pastorate of the Rev. W. Veale, and more than eighty members were added to the church.   Previous to this the membership had dwindled down to nine persons.   This revival soon caused the church to be too small so it was decided to rebuild.   A new deed was drawn up on July 17th, 1890 and the names on it were J. Edmonds, James Penrose, S. Osborne, W. Veale, R. B. Slee-man, T. Moffatt, N. Pearse, and A. Ralph.   The chapel was rebuilt on the old site in 1896, and a schoolroom added.   During the building of it the congregation held their services in the Reform Chapel.   The pastor of the Bible Christian Church at this time was the Rev. John Page.

In 1841 the Rev. N. F. Chudleigh was appointed Incumbent of the Parish of St. Columb Minor.   At that time the majority of the parishioners lived in Newquay.   He saw at once the difficulty of visiting or caring for those of his church successfully over such a scattered area.   This was not a pleasant outlook for any young vicar, especially when he saw how impossible it would be for the aged and delicate to attend any of the services held in the Parish Church.   Then there were the very young—the future hope of the church—to be considered. How little we of to-day imagine what those must have passed through when faced with such obstacles.

A few years later the Rev. C. H. Hutton, D.D., came to reside in Newquay and he saw the needs of the children of the working classes, as well as the disabilities of the aged and infirm.   He hired the drying loft of the somewhat dilapidated old malthouse which formerly stood opposite Primrose House in Gover Lane.   The loft had been divided and the half facing the town was used as a dwelling house, up to a few years ago. It was the inner half that Dr. Hutton rented for his school and   services—(the same in which Mr. William Moyses in 1850 had his school).   This went on for a time and each year the number of visitors to the town was increasing.   Among those who came in 1857 was a Mrs. Carpenter of Tavistock, Devon.   This lady felt the lack of a regular church service in the midst of such a growing population, and she mentioned

the matter to Mr. Chudleigh with the offer that she would
head a subscription list with £100 if he would move in the direction of building a church.   Mr. Chudleigh was delighted with
the idea and at once set to work.   Subscriptions from landowners and others came in and William Michell, Esq., offered
to give the site.   This so encouraged the Vicar and people
that the foundation stone was laid on March 17th, 1858 by Mrs.
Michell.   I sang in the impromptu choir, and was intensely
interested in watching Mrs. Michell's use of the trowel.   Dr.
Hutton as well as Dr. Pusey took a keen interest in the work
and they seemed to communicate their earnestness to the
general public.

Thus the building of the church went steadily on, until
on Sept. 9th, 1858, the Chapel of Ease or Church of St. Michael
was opened and consecrated for Divine worship.   It consisted of chancel and nave and seated about 200.   The singing
was led by Mr. John James, with his flute for the first year or so.
The accommodation was after a time found to be inadequate
and in 1873 a north aisle was added and the west end extended.
A small spire was also built at this time.

Further improvements were effected in 1881 and a south
aisle, organ chamber, and vestry were added thus utilising
the whole site.   The church could now accommodate 550.

Each year was marked by an increase of visitors, and in
1905 it was felt necessary to procure a new site.   This was
purchased from the Michell Estate Trustees for £525.   The
raising of funds sufficient to build a church such as was required
must have meant strenuous efforts for those who undertook
it.   The contributions which came in so stimulated the workers that on Sept. 7th, 1909, the foundation stone of the present
church was laid by Mrs. Arthur Tremayne.

———————

In 1874 the crowded state of the graveyard at the Parish
Church of St. Columb Minor made it necessary to extend the
burial ground.

Moreover the greater part of the population of the parish was resident in Newquay so that it became desirable that Newquay should obtain a burial ground of its own.

Up to this time, when there was a funeral, the coffin had to be carried to St. Columb Minor church by hand, there being no hearse in the town. If the weather was wet covered vehicles would be provided for the women and children who invariably attended funerals in those days. It may seem strange now but women acted as bearers for women and girls.

I remember as a child, the funeral of a very beautiful woman who was only twenty-one years of age, and had been married but a year. Her bearers were eight young women dressed in white. According to the usual custom the body was brought out of the house and the friends standing around sang a hymn. Then the little company slowly moved through the town and so by Marky's Hill to Narrowcliff and St. Columb Minor.

Such was the impression made on my childish mind at these funerals that even now, in passing through Lower St. Columb, I invariably listen for the tolling of the bell.

At a public meeting it was decided that Newquay should acquire its own burial ground, so two Burial Boards were formed, one for the Parish and one for the Local Board district of Newquay. The Rev. N. F. Chudleigh was chosen chairman for the Parish and Mr. W. E. Michell chairman for Newquay. About half-an-acre of land was purchased from the Duchy of Cornwall.

The day appointed for the consecration of the first, or what is now known as the old cemetery, was January 1st, 1875. The Bishop of Exeter (Dr. Temple) performed the ceremony. He was accompanied by the Rev. Chancellor Phillpots, and attended by his secretary. A considerable number of people were present and the clergy who attended the Revs. N. F. Chudleigh, vicar, R. Mildren, curate, and M. Maurice, vicar of Crantock. There was a large marquee erected on the church portion of the cemetery for the consecration service. I was present with the family of the vicar of

Crantock. It was a cold day and a shower came on just as the ceremony was concluded. The Bishop, not caring to get wet before reaching his carriage, told his chaplain to " look sharp and hurry up,"which was, as one of those present remarked, a very " unbishop like" expression !

The pretty sheltered Lych Gate was erected from plans made by Mr. John Ennor.

CHAPTER XIX

WELL-KNOWN INHABITANTS

WE must not forget that no place is ever built up merely by its more prominent inhabitants. At the most the latter, possessing a large amount of leisure, can devote time to the more conspicuous part of social life. But the former —the actual makers of prosperity—are often less noticeable publicly by reason of the very exacting nature of their occupations.

It is of these people that I shall write in the present chapter, and of them Richard Carne was the earliest I remember.

Richard Carne was born in 1807 at St. Columb Minor and learnt the carpentering with his father, John Carne, who built the round part of the Tower for Captain Frederick Rogers, R.N., when he acquired the land in 1835.

Some years after Mr. Gregor, of Trewarthenick, bought the Tower and grounds, and employed Richard Carne, who was then in business for himself in Newquay, to add the two square portions. Later, when the Tower became the property of Sir Paul Molesworth, he was again employed to build the wing which was used as the private chapel for the family. He built the Retreat overlooking the harbour, and Eveningside, the first detached house on the Mount Wise estate. In 1852 he built the Wesleyan Chapel. The two three-storied houses called Adelaide Place were also built by him. They are now converted into shops, one of which is occupied by W. H. Smith & Sons, Booksellers. Criddle and Smith now occupy two shops whichCarne erected in his garden. The first six houses in Acland Terrace were also built by him. Two of the apprentices he trained—Mr. John Ennor and Mr. C. Bellingham—became successful builders in the town.

Richard Carne was a tall, dark, handsome man, with clear blue eyes, a born musician and singer. He trained and led the first choir in the then new Wesleyan Chapel, where for many years he played the 'cello.

When 28 years of age he married the daughter of Captain Enedor Billing. They had eight children, Thomas, John, Richard, William, Tryphena, Elizabeth, Maria and Mary. Through the kindness of Miss Mary Carne of 6, Acland Terrace, I obtained the following from their family tree, which was arranged and copied by Sir Paul Molesworth from Mrs. Gregor's MSS. Their descent is traced from the Kings of Cornwall, of whom Ithael was slain A.D. 846. Then followed the names of several other kings. The first part of the history is taken from the Glamorgan branch, showing the arms and descent of the Carnes.

The family name is still to be found at Cowbridge in Glamorgan. The later part of the history given on the tree was taken from the Baptismal Register of St. Columb Minor.

In the reign of Elizabeth a family of Carnes settled here and still exist, claiming to be descendants from the Carnes of Glamorgan, and adduced as proof of the truth of the family traditions the fact that, until the alterations in the Church of St. Columb Minor, the bench ends of their pew had upon it the Carne Arms—a Pelican feeding her young from her own breast. With regard to the use of the arms, the antiquary, Sir John Maclean, in 1873 said that no such assumption of arms could have been allowed in ancient times unless the party assuming them could show their right to them.

From the register the following names are given— Roger Carne 1585, Robert 1608, Robert 1649, Thomas 1688, John 1714, who was parish clerk for 50 years, dying in 1801. John 1764, father of Richard, who was born 1807, and died 1880, aged 73 years.

The family of Billings came originally from Brittany and settled in Newquay. Enedor, Mrs. Carne's father, was baptised at the Parish Church of St. Columb Minor, May 29th, 1779. He was one of thirteen sons. After his wife died he went to live with the Carnes and died July 11th, 1844.

GRANNY BILLING'S COTTAGE.

When Mrs. Carne was about six years old he asked Mr. R. Lomax if his little Betsy might ride in his carriage, as it was the first she had ever seen drawn by a pair of horses ; so Betsy had her ride.

Mr. Lomax, when at Newquay, always lodged with Mrs. R. Billing (Granny Billing) in the large old house on the town side of Rose Cellars, South Quay Hill. Enedor was Captain of one of the Newquay schooners. He learnt navigation and traded in the Mediterranean and Black Sea. The life of a sailor in those days was very exciting. During one of his voyages he was taken prisoner by the French, and those at home had an anxious tine until he was liberated. Richard Billing, in 1838, was granted a lease for 99 years on Rose Cellars, also on his house and meadow mentioned above. At the same time his brotherWilliam had a lease for 99 years granted to him on the Island on the Town Beach.

It would be interesting to know how the Island passed out of the hands of the Billings, seeing that their lease does not expire till 1937. I have often seen the Billing brothers at work in their garden on the Island, and I also have a dim recollection of a controversy going on in the Town respecting the Island property, and some other folks than the Billings laying claim to it.

Enedor also had a new enclosure of ten poles for building purposes on a lease of 99 years.

The Billings appear to have been an enterprising family and to have acquired land at every opportunity.

About 1800 Mr. John Bunt came from Palperro to Newquay. He was one of the first coast-guards sent here to watch smugglers. In his early life he had been a sailor, and in those days any civilian of good report could become a coastguard.

John did his work so efficiently that he gained the confidence of those in authority and in course of time became commander of one of the cutters.

His children were Mary, Nancy, Sally, John, Robert, and Jenny, and when they grew up naturally looked around for partners. Seeing there were few inhabitants in Newquay except those engaged in seafaring, fishing or smuggling, the natural consequence was that the children of the watchers must, if they married at all, become allied with the families of the watched !

Mary, the eldest, kept a dame school for awhile ; then married William Osborne, a leading bargeman in the Gannel. Nancy married Tailor Green, Sally became the wife of Tommy Osborne the quarryman, while Robert married Betsy Billing. All the family were middle-aged people when I was a child, but I remember them quite well.

Robert became a coastguard, and, like all others up to that date, had to seek a house where he could, as none was provided by the authorities as is the case at the present time.

In 1825 the coastguard buildings were erected. It was quite a new thing to see a row of houses built at the same time, and for many years they were spoken of as " the buildings." Robert and Betsy were among the first to live in the coastguard cottages.

Robert told me of a little dodge they used for resting when on their long tramps around the coast at night. Inside their coats they carried a small flat piece of wood, and also a wooden peg about fourteen inches long sharpened at one end to stick into the ground. On the other end, which was flat, rested the other piece of wood, so that a somewhat precarious seat was made. It was impossible to sleep on such an insecure support and thus they avoided detection on any surprise visit.

After some time Robert was removed to the South East Coast, but not liking it he left the service and decided to return to his native place. Robert and his wife came as far as Exeter by train and walked the remainder of the journey, as funds were low.

When they came to cross the ferry at Saltash they were penniless. Robert suggested that they should tell the ferryman and trust to his good nature to take them across. Betsy said, " No ! Robert. That will never do. The man will not

take us if he knows we can't pay. We must go on board as if
it was quite the regular thing to cross ferries and, when we get
out on the other side, tell the man we are sorry, but are penniless and will pay him when we return !"

Betsy always told the yarn as though it was a joy to her
to remember it. The man's expression and language made her
sorry that others were not present to enjoy the fun !

Robert and Betsy were a remarkable couple. He was
clever and, for his generation, well educated, but was not as
concerned about ways and means as he should have been.
His wife always had to manage the purse to keep their young
family clothed and fed. She was a dressmaker and tailoress,
and even in those days of low wages managed to keep things
going.

After their return, Robert set up a school at Cubert in the
old chapel where John Wesley preached on the many occasions
when he visited his old friend, Mr. Joseph Hosken, of Carines
House. The chapel stands on the right hand corner at the
entrance of the village from Crantock.

After a time Robert gave up his school, possibly because
either the scholars were too few or the daily journey from
Newquay too irksome.

In those days many of our vessels were laid up during
the winter months and quite a number of the captains and
sailors spent their time in study. This was Robert's opportunity. He suggested their taking courses of lessons in navigation as well as in ordinary subjects.

He rented the old count house at Mount Wise and started
a school there. I knew many married captains and sailors
as well as younger men who attended. It was Robert who
gave Lehenver Mine the new name of Mount Wise. During
the summer he and his wife were engaged in other work.

He knew something of music too, his favourite instrument being the flute. I remember him coming to our house
of an evening when I was a child, and playing while the others
sang.

After we had removed to Crantock Mrs. Bunt used to come over for three or four days at a time to sew. On one occasion my sister and I had agreed to bring her across the Gannel in our boat.

Unfortunately the tide had turned and the wind was blowing strongly out of the Gannel. Our difficulty was to prevent the boat from being carried below Penpol Point, but Mrs. Bunt knew nothing of this until we had landed at Penpol Quay and told her how anxious we had been.

Very complacently she said, " How very interesting it would have been if our boat had been carried out of the Gannel. Then the lifeboat would have had to come after us ! What a sensation it would have caused in the town !" I must say we had no wish to participate in such a sensation !

John, the son of John and Betsy Ennor, was born at Newquay on February 13th, 1828. A very tragic event left him fatherless when he was only three years old.

His father was supervising for Mr. Richard Lomax the clearing of the foundation for the construction of the South Pier.

One night it was an exceptionally high tide and he went down to see that all was right. After waiting long and anxiously, Mary Moyses took charge of the baby while Mrs. Ennor went down to the Quay to look for her husband, but alas ! without success.

He must have slipped off the wall in the dark, as his body was found next day washed up in the cove at the back of the Pier.

Like so many of our brave women in former days she faced the difficulties and did the best she could for her boy.

Mrs. Ennor was an excellent singer. When she was very old, Mrs. Prout, my mother, my sister and I went out to her house to see her one Christmas and sang several carols. She was delighted and specially thanked the two " dear children " for coming to sing to her. She had a sitting in our seat in the Baptist Chapel and it was often my privilege to sit next her. She had a nice, high footstool and I was allowed to stand on this when the hymns were sung. I should think from what I remember of her that she must have been very fond of children. She bound her boy, John, an apprentice to Richard Carne. After completing his indentures his first important piece of work was to put in the gallery in the Methodist chapel. This was in 1849. Soon after this he went to London to gain experience, and came back, in 1855 or 6 to begin in real earnest his life's work. In 1877 he built the Railway Station and between that date and December, 1890, he had erected ninety houses in Newquay. He married and had a family of three children, a son and two daughters. They all settled in Newquay : his son John became a very successful surveyor, and laid out the East Pentire Estate.

It may be said that the Ennors for four generations have been the pioneers in the laying-out and helping to build up modern Newquay. Mr. Ennor's speculations showed his unbounded confidence in the future growth of the town.

He was the local agent to the Treffry Estate for several years and a member of the Local Board for twenty years, taking a keen interest in all public affairs. He was one of the first members of the Loyal Fort Lodge of Oddfellows and held the office of Treasurer for over 30 years. Amongst his other activities, the fishing industries claimed his generous support. He renewed the leases of the Active, the Fly, and Good Intent concerns.

Mr. Ennor took a keen interest in shipping and owned shares in several vessels and was a member of the Newquay Mutual Marine Shipping Association. His favourite recreation was boating, and in later years could often be seen sailing his yacht in the Bay.

He was a devoted member of the Wesleyan Society, a class leader, and a trustee. Not long after the present Wesleyan Church was built he presented the society with an individual communion service. He passed away on Monday, Feb. 11th, 1912, aged 84 years within two days.

Mr. James Pearce was born in Newquay and educated under Mr. Stephens, a clever man and a strict disciplinarian.

He became a leading Cornish farmer, and owned or rented several farms in the neighbourhood of Newquay. He was specially keen on dairy cows and went to the Channel Islands two or three times to secure the pure breed for dairy purposes. Often during the season he had sixty cows in milk. Although he had such an extensive business he devoted both time and energy to municipal affairs. He was a Free Trader and a Liberal and took a keen interest in politics. He was chairman of the Local Board for many years and when the Urban Council was formed he was again elected chairman and remained in office four years. He became a member of the Cornwall County Council, and represented the Newquay Division for three years. As a Councillor he was held in high esteem for his integrity and sound judgment. Being of a bright disposition and even-tempered he had a great advantage in many heated discussions that took place in the Council Chamber. He was always anxious to do his best so that Newquay might be in a position to vie with other watering places. Mr. Pearce was a staunch Nonconformust, a strict Baptist, but a liberal supporter of any work undertaken for the uplifting and general welfare of the people.

He married Grace, third daughter of Robert Nicholls, Esq., of St. Pinnock, brought up a large family and died on May May 19th, 1908, at his residence, Lehenver Villa.

CHAPTER XX

PUBLIC HOUSES AND MALTHOUSES.

I N 1800 the Old Inn stood in what is now known as the Central Square. From its general appearance in 1855 as I knew it when a girl, the inn must have been two or three hundred years old and well deserved the appellation, " The Old Inn." It was by no means a pretentious looking house, and yet, including the Town Hall, it occupied all the site on which the Central Hotel now stands.

There was nothing about it to denote a broken down or ill kept appearance : in fact there was a general air of respectability attached to the place.

The landlady, Mrs. Parkyn, too, was a well set up woman, and looked quite capable of conducting her own business. Her husband, William, was a boot and shoe maker, and he and his man worked in the room over the double doors. This workshop was entered from the back yard.

The long room extending from the workshop to the end of the building on the right was the Town Hall. This too was entered from the back yard. In the Town Hall were held lectures, entertainments, bazaars and other public meetings.

According to present needs it could scarcely be said to be entirely suitable,but we were satisfied—and what else mattered ?

There were some features common to all the old public houses, so that one general description will apply to all. To every one was attached a brewhouse. No chemicals were used in those days. The beer was made of pure malt and hops. Each public house had a special man for this work. He was the brewer and acted as ostler as well. Jimmy George was always associated with the Old Inn and seemed as important to the conduct of the general affairs of the Inn as did Mrs. Parkyn herself.

The Central Square.

The public house had a brew-day each week and two days later would be the barm—or yeast day. In those good old thrifty days every housewife baked her own bread and cake (saffron of course !) This was done in a large earthenware oven built into the kitchen chimney. Sending for the barm was thus necessary for every household and so it was essential that we should know when all the brewing operations took place. It was no unusual sight to see a hundred or so little jugs of all shapes and sizes and colours arranged on a table in the brewhouse waiting to be filled with barm. Then there was a general bustle when people came to claim their own jugs of barm.

All the inns had a large yard at the back or side. It was called the " backlet" and in it was situated the brewhouse, and all the washing of barrels and brew-tubs took place there. The stables and coach-houses were also in the yard.

Attached to each inn was a long skittle alley. Skittles was a fine recreation, and on summer evenings, when the playing was in full swing, many people would assemble to watch the game. I have often wondered why such a graceful game should have fallen so much into disuse ; in the full play of every muscle and precision of movement it certainly compares very favourably with any other game.

In those days every farm house, which had apprentice boys, had its own skittle alley. I have played at Tregunnel and also at Trevella with the children of the family and the farm hands.

Another very old public house was the Shipwright Arms. This house is now known as Cliff Cottage and is situated opposite the Red Lion Hotel. In 1800 it was kept by a man named Massey and was licensed to sell beer and porter only. Massey was a shipwright by trade, and built his boats in a long shed in the open yard between the end of his house and Harbour Terrace. At that time the Shipwright Arms was the only public house near the Quay and was frequented by sailors and fishermen. I remember as a child often going into the yard on my way to school in Harbour Terrace. There was an enormously deep well in the yard : the water was drawn up by windlass and kibble. Tregurrian House now occupies the site of the yard.

The Ship Inn was situated where now stands Messrs. Huxtables' Stores at the back of the Central Square. The Victoria Hall stands on the site of the old backlet of this inn. After the brew-day was over the malt grains were used by the landlord to mix with the ordinary food for the pigs. It was no unusual sight to see the pigs lying about in various stages of intoxication, after having eaten too freely, and pig-like were utterly helpless until the fumes passed off.

The skittle alley attached to the Ship Inn extended from the end of the house to Wesley Hill Road. It was outside the hedge that enclosed the backlet. This was an advantage to the children, because they were free to watch the games played there. The proprietor, Mr. Trevithick, was rather a superior looking man and one of whom no advantage was likely to be taken. On the hedge of the backlet down Wesley Hill grew large bushes of Elder. It was quite a pretty sight when the bushes were in full bloom. These Elder bushes were known locally as " skewtrees," because the hard part of the wood was cut into short lengths and made into skewers and used by the butchers in dressing meat.

The New Inn, paradoxical as it may seem, appeared nearly as old as the other inns mentioned. It has been very much modernised and it is now known as the New Hotel. In thinking of the inn as it used to be one can scarcely recognise the new building. The front door was in the gable end facing the Central Square. In the front wall, facing the street, were two very small deep-set windows downstairs and two upstairs. So deep-set were they that anyone coming toward the house could scarcely realise there were any windows in that side of the inn. On the whole of the space from the house to Church Lane stood the backlet, which was entered through a large gate by the side of the house. In this were

the usual stables, brewhouse and skittle alley. Mr. Cock
was the landlord. He was generally engaged on his farm,
Mrs. Cock managing the affairs of the house. They kept a
dairy and sold the milk and cream to regular customers
who came for it. In those days none of the inns were run
apart from some other business, because the amount of
trade would not of itself be sufficient to keep the family.

One little amusing incident might be mentioned in
connection with the New Inn. A man was sent from Porth
with a two-gallon jar for beer. For convenience he carried
it on his back in a sack. He met a kindred spirit and so
they had a drink together. Then the jar was filled and off
he went with his load. But the strong Newquay air seemed
to affect him and when he came to the Barrow Fields the
stile seemed to rise before him ! He tried to get the better
of the stile, which was, however, too much for him and down
he came on the other side with the jar bang on the top step.
Result—broken jar—spilt beer. But, nothing daunted, he
shouldered his bag and went on. When he arrived he lifted
down the bag with great care saying to his mistress, '' Aw,
Missus I've brok the jar. But tes all in the bag !''

The Red Lion was built in 1835 by Mrs. Thomas, who en
closed the land in 1831 on a 99 year lease. She must have
been a far-seeing woman to have decided upon building such
a large house when, as far as one could see, there was no
demand for it. Her idea evidently was to cater for the
future. She must have felt that Newquay would grow
and become a residential and fashionable watering place.
In this, we know, her hopes were fulfilled. The addition
of a verandah some years ago has been the only addition
to the hotel proper. The yard at the back has been built on
to make extra accommodation for servants. Of course in
those early days of visitors coming to Newquay many of
them were accommodated in private rooms at the inns,
and I feel sure they would have nothing to complain of
from the attention given to them on their visits.

One of the landlords of the Red Lion told me the following story.

An amusing little altercation took place between him and one of his customers concerning the running up of a long " score." The customer disputed the amount he had to pay and the landlord decided to teach him a lesson. The landlord, who was a ship builder had, in his pocket, a piece of chalk which had been used for rubbing over the cord when marking lines on the wood. The middle of the chalk was consequently worn down by the cord leaving two projections. With this chalk he showed the man that he could make two marks at one stroke when marking up the score behind the cellar door, and suggested that this could not be done if the drink were paid for when ordered. This little ruse was successful in stopping the man going into debt for beer.

———

One of the minor industries in 1800 was malting, which gave employment to several men as the kilns had to be watched night and day. As this was one of the essentials connected with inns and brewing a brief account will be put here.

There were six houses in or near the town. One was situated on the left-hand side of Quay House and is now incorporated into the dwelling house. The Malthouse in Alma Place is still in a fairly good state of preservation. In 1860 it was used as a school.

In 1870 I remember attending a lecture there. The subject was " The finding of Livingstone by Stanley." There were two malt houses in Gover Lane. One stood on the site where Fern Bank Villa new stands and another opposite Primrose House. It has quite recently been taken down. There is another still in a good state of preservation at Tregunnel.

The greater part of the barley grown in the neighbourhood was converted into malt at these houses.

The malthouse at Trenance stands on the left side of the road overlooking the Public Gardens. Sometime ago it was converted into cottages and is an ideal spot for those who like a sheltered spot. Contrasted with the wild coast on the north Trenance is really a picture of quiet rural beauty with its sylvan lanes hidden deep down in the hollow, and with its picturesque cottages, leafy thickets, and trickling streams, is a truly glorious spot.

CHAPTER XXI

———

THE GANNEL CRAKE.

IN writing of the Gannel Crake I have no pet theory to advance, as to what it is, or what produces the sounds. Some, who have never heard it, settle the question at once by saying it is some strange bird visiting the Gannel on rare occasions. Others say the sounds are produced by the inrush of water in some deep cavern near. My object is to state simple facts, as I have had them from those whose word, as I estimate it, is beyond question.

It was the time of landing sea weed, the rank deep sea weed which washes on shore once a year and is known as the weed harvest. It was collected by farmers and their men as soon as the tide receded sufficiently and piled in heaps above high water mark to be taken to the fields at a more leisurely time of the year and used as manure.

On this particular morning two young men, with two horses and a cart, were busy at work on Crantock Beach just below the steps, leading down from West Pentire. One was raking up the weed and the other was loading the cart. Suddenly the most unearthly noise began, the horses took fright and galloped in over the beach. The men ran across the Green and caught them and led them back to their work but they found it difficult to quiet them after their excitement. I asked one of the men what he thought it was. " It was like nothing I had ever heard before," said he, " It was like a thousand voices in pent-up misery with one long drawn wail dying away in the distance." He did not entertain the idea of its being a bird : it was in broad daylight, and the bird, if there had been one, could have been seen. The sound seemed to be right over their heads. He had many times heard the corn-crake, but it was nothing like this.

Just opposite the Fern Pit a vessel lay up against the bar of sand and a barge had been loaded from her and was awaiting the incoming tide to be taken to Trevemper Bridge for unloading. One of the men was coming up from the little cabin when the weird cry of the Crake sounded so near his head that he dropped back into the cabin, so unexpected was the sound, and then he heard the wail dying away out into the Gannel. This man was bound an apprentice as bargeman so had spent most of his young life on the Gannel, and was well accustomed to all birds visiting there both night and day. This was the first time he had ever heard the crake, but he heard it again, two or three times after. He never saw anything that would help him solve the mystery as to what produced the sound.

On another occasion a father, daughter and friend, went part of the way to Crantock to escort an elderly friend safely across the Gannel one evening. They went as far as Penpol House and were returning and descending to the sands at Penpol Point when they heard the Crake. Neither of them had ever before heard it and they were all terribly frightened—too scared to speak or suggest what it could be. I expect the climbing of Trethellan Hill was a sprint in record time for them ! When they arrived at Newquay, the friend, before any explanation could be given, fell on the floor in a dead faint. It is difficult to conceive what a great impression it must have made on all three. As they told us afterwards the cry was too awful for words.

About 1872 we were living at Crantock, and the Doctor had to be fetched from Newquay one night. He came at about 10 o'clock and after seeing the patient, came downstairs and sat for a chat, as he often did, but this night he seemed unusually quiet. At last he said to mother, " Have you ever heard the Crake Mrs. H. ?" " No," she answered, " But you have." " Well," he said, " I don't know, but to-night, coming through Penpol Quay it was such a lovely night I let the reins hang loosely on the horse's neck, and was enjoying the quiet restfulness of the place, when, all at once, just overhead, I heard such a sound as I shall never forget. It passed on up through the Trevithick Valley and so went trailing away in the distance."

I don't think in either of the cases I have mentioned was there any thought of the crake in the minds of those who heard it. It came on them when least expected and, very likely, if those same friends had been asked before if they believed in the crake they would have laughed at the idea.

In 1916 I called to see a friend at Pentire. Her house stands on the Gannel side, near the old farm house. We were chatting some time when all at once she said, " We have heard the crake ! I know you take a keen interest in all that pertains to Newquay. About a week ago two friends had called, and were taking lunch with us. I think the crake or anything connected with the Gannel was the furthest thing from our thoughts, when all at once all conversationn stopped and we looked at each other and simultaneously said, ' It must be the crake.' We rose from the table, went to the window, and looked up and down the Gannel. All was quiet and there was nothing unusual to be seen."

It was the same unearthly troubled sound that startled them. I said it was the first account I had had of any one hearing it on the Pentire Estate, but they knew of others hearing it. However fear of being laughed at prevented them from mentioning it generally.

Some will say that it is heard less frequently now than formerly, but that is accounted for by the fact that comparatively few people now are on the Gannel night or day, whereas fifty years ago the Gannel was never free from people engaged either in shipping or barging. The cases I have mentioned occurred at varying times in the day or night. If the theory of its being a bird is taken it could hardly be a night and a day bird. Again, why was it never seen ? It has been suggested to me that it might be a frigate bird, and that on rare occasions one might come so far north. To me it is still a mystery, but that it does exist, and was heard by all those I have mentioned, I have not the slightest doubt.

CHAPTER XXII.

———

LOST LANDMARKS

HARBOUR OF REFUGE.

O F all the lost landmarks connected with the Newquay of the past the unfinished Harbour of Refuge is the most to be deplored.

To the west of the isthmus leading to the Headland is to be seen a piece of solid masonry, which is all that remains of the first Pier of the much-needed harbour of refuge which was projected by Mr. Treffry.

THE HARBOUR OF REFUGE.

Many a time, when a child, have I run up and down this pier and over the steps, or watched the men pushing the little waggons along the railway under the bridge from the rocks on the Newquay side of the isthmus.

Staging was erected across the new harbour to form a temporary viaduct so that the waggons could be run on to the pier. The huge blocks of granite were brought from Luxulyan by the then new railway to the Newquay Harbour and were shipped on flat-bottomed boats. These were rowed across the Gazel to the rocks and the granite was then hoisted into the waggons by a derrick which had been erected on a staging. There seemed to be such a wonderful amount to watch in all this undertaking.

The main Pier was completed and the men were engaged in blasting the rocks in the centre of the harbour as well as on the Little Fistral side of the area to be enclosed. The powder for blasting was stored in a little cave on the right-hand side of the road leading down into the harbour. The plan was to make a large sheltered harbour available at all states of the tide, by cutting through the narrow neck of land separating the two bays. However, this enterprise was abruptly terminated and what the ravages of time and tide have left of the pier stands there as a monument of what might have been had Mr. Treffry lived or had others taken up the work. How little can we estimate the far-reaching benefit to shipping generally if such a Refuge had been completed!

––––––

The Bark House.

There are some things associated in the mind with certain places or objects that to mention such awakens the memory of other days. The old Bark House is one such object.

From its appearance it must have been very old even when I was a child. But now even its site is lost to view, being covered with sheds and stores. In the old days, however, it was a most interesting spot when the preparations for the fishing season were in full swing.

The bringing of the bark, bound in large bundles piled in waggons, the fire under the immense furnace in which the bark was boiled, the nets being laid in the long troughs, the pouring of the fragrant bark over the nets, the men watching with critical eyes to see that the dyeing colour was correct, and then the nets being taken out in their rich brown new dress—all these things were of absorbing interest.

The spent bark was thrown in a heap outside and was free to the public. It was used as a backing for slow burning fires.

The nets when taken out were spread on the grass-covered mounds of blown sand in the Bark-house field to dry. When children we loved to run over the nets, and if our feet caught in the meshes, down we went rolling over the steep mounds to be further entangled as we rolled. Then came the men and women to mend the nets on bright sunny days. There was a fascination in watching this work that we could not resist. The women wore little turnovers (shawls) over their shoulders and their drawn lilac sun bonners were quite picturesque. The two leading women at the work were Mrs. Betsy Bunt and Mrs. Mary Betty Ellery. All the others worked under their direction. It was a feast for the eyes to see the swiftly moving shuttle filling up the holes. Sometimes large patches of net had to be meshed in, but the deft way they joined it all and made the net complete rendered it quite a work of art.

THE CANNON.

Many years after the Spanish Armada was scattered and the galleons driven ashore on the coasts of our islands, two cannons were found in the Bay near the entrance to Porth. The Porth folks claimed one of them and Newquay the other. Ours was brought home and placed on the Commons, on the sand dunes, between Wesley Hill and the Squire's yard.

As time went on the sand was carried away week by week by the children of the town for sanding the floors, the cannon gradually sank into the sand pit. So that particular pit was spoken of by the children as the cannon pit and later it became customary to call all that part of the Common the Cannon Pit.

After some years, when most of the sand had been removed, someone hit on a bright idea—that of taking the cannon from its long resting place and carrying it on to the Beacon, there to be used on Regatta Days for starting the different races.   It was placed on a rocky ledge just below the road, about midway leading to the Huer's House. This answered splendidly for a time, and when the reverberating echoes sounded across the bay it added somewhat to the dignity of the occasion.

This, however, was not allowed to go on long. One summer night, some young gentlemen (?) visitors saw in it not a memento of the Spanish Armada or a cannon to be used for pleasure in starting races at Regattas, but a *toy* for their childish play, and in their wantonness, having nothing better to do, they rolled it down the slope on to the rocks, and into the cove below, where it soon became embedded in the sand.   It would certainly be an act of great generosity if some person or persons would volunteer to bear the expense of raising it to its former position on the Beacon.

THE ANCHOR.

The anchor was found and brought ashore by Mr. John Clemens of Prospect House, long   after the cannon had found its resting place on the Common.   From the make of the anchor it was considered to be of Spanish workmanship, and no doubt belonged to one of the galleons that was driven before the gale in 1588.   It lay in Mr. Clemens' ship-building yard disregarded and apparently valueless for a time. When Fairfax F. Ivimey, Esq., took up his residence here, he showed a keen desire to know something of the past life of the people, and there were those ready to satisfy, as far as they could, that desire. Hence the anchor was spoken of and brought to his notice. He expressed a wish to have it preserved as a relic, and offered a resting-place for it in the grounds at the Fort. This thoughtful act must be appreciated by all those who have a love for old associations.

THE LOOK-OUT HOUSE.

The demolition of the Look-out House will ever remain a source of deep regret to some of the old inhabitants.

I venture to say that if those boys who went forth to the Great War and gave their lives for their country had been consulted, they would have pleaded for its retention, and suggested some other spot on which to rear a war memorial. It was associated with their earliest boyhood days : around it they played ; they climbed its steps ; they looked out over the Atlantic from its roofledge. It seemed almost a part of their home life, and in their different occupations in after years, when nearing home, either by sea or land, it was the first object they sighted, and would thrill them with the thought of home. Sir Robert Edgcumbe was imbued with the right spirit when he made his magnificent offer to purchase it and hand it over to the Society for the Preservation of Ancient Buildings. Nothing seemed to weigh with the Executive Committee : they had determined to carry out their own ideas. But there is one redeeming feature : they were not natives, so possibly could not sympathise with native wishes or aspirations.

The Look-out House was built to commemorate our victory in the European Wars of a century ago. It was used by the coast guards as a look-out and shelter until the present signal station was built.

As far as one can see there was nothing to prevent its being purchased by the town and treasured as a relic of antiquity.

CHAPTER XXIII.

OLD GARDENS

SOME have fancied our life in those far-off days must
have been fraught with many an anxious moment,
seeing there was no Doctor near at hand to minister the
healing balm when required ; but we were Nature's children,
and living close to Nature had learnt of her secrets.

Many of our women knew the art of curing by means of
herbs, and herbs are Nature's remedies. It is well for us
to remember that the founders of Medical Science were
herbalists and the curative properties of medicine prescribed
to-day are more herbal than anything else. The only difference is that the doctor prescribes the drug extracts, while the
herbalist makes a tea by infusing the herb.

Much was said and written in 1914, at the commence-
ment of the war, on the lost art of cultivating herbs in England. At that time our foreign imports in medical plants
alone were costing us thousands of pounds each year, all of
which we could have saved by growing the same plants at
home as our grand-parents did up to the middle of the
nineteenth century. It was wonderful the interest taken in
herb-growing and flower culture all through my early life
in Newquay.

One man I knew went every year to Cubert Commons,
round Trezean and Treworguns, to collect herbs grown in that
neighbourhood and came back at night laden with his spoils.
These were spread in the sun and turned each day until dry ;
then put in large paper bags, labelled and hung up in what was
known as the " spense," which meant, I suppose, " dispensary." In the immediate neighbourhood, elder-blossom,
meadow-sweet, horehound, dandelion, and monkshood were
culled and dried in the same way and kept for winter use.
Most of the cottages had a garden attached to them and every
inch of ground had to produce something ; any waste or rough

bits were filled with herbs. In one garden I have seen growing such herbs as foxgloves, valerian, camomile, opium poppy, peppermint, marigolds, sweet lavender, sage and thyme.

As the camomile flowers opened they were picked off and spread for drying. I was told once, when helping to do this, to be careful, as every single head was worth sixpence. In this same garden there was a choice assortment of old-time flowers to send forth their fragrance as well as to please the eye. Crocus, daffodils, primroses, polyanthus, hyacinths, fuchsias, forget-me-nots, mignonette, geraniums, everlasting peas, myrtle, larkspurs, salvia, currant rivis, and hydrangea. Near the door of the cottage was an arch of laburnum and lilac intertwined—how I loved to watch for the hanging golden tassels and the purple wealth of flowers of those two trees. Then the roses—all old-fashioned—monthly roses, cabbage, white, York and Lancaster roses, moss rose and sweetbriar —they were all in this same garden, and one felt an indescribable stillness pervading everything there, and as I think of it now it seems almost like a fairy scene.

This was only one of the many gardens in old Newquay. There were others larger, containing fruit trees. Mrs. Vivian's garden was an ideal spot for choice fruit ; so also was Mr. W. Carrivick's and Mrs. Marshall's. Then, too, there was Mr. John Reynolds' orchard, situated in the triangular piece of ground between Beach Road and Gover Lane, the site now being occupied by the Council Buildings. To stand at the foot of Wesley Hill and look down over the orchard when in full bloom was one of the most perfect pictures one could wish to see.

Mr. Thomas Osborne told me that in the old garden where the Wesleyan Chapel was built in 1852, they grew such a number of crocuses that one year there were so many that his mother dried them and was able to make her own cakes from the saffron obtained from them.

The planting of trees, too, was not forgotten. There are a few still left to remind the present generation that trees can be grown in and around the town.   The four or five in Beach Road looked old to me seventy years ago, and yet they are still there, although exposed to the force of the winter gales.   Near the Baptist Chapel there are three or four **Poplar** trees, which were planted nearly a hundred years ago **and** still remain.   In another spot just over the Harbour a **stray** sycamore seed settled in Captain W. Dark's garden and took root and has grown so that in summer it provides a welcome shade to the front of the house.

Privet, hawthorn and tamarisk need very little culture to form pretty flowering hedges.   When the Tower was built the whole length of the boundary hedge was planted with tamarisk, which formed a fine fence and looked well whilst kept trim.   It made a pleasant picture when in bloom —the slender feathery branchlets clothed with minute, closely packed leaves intermingled with the small tasselled pink and white flowers.

Although sensitive to frost yet it will flourish to perfection in our hedgerows, no matter how exposed the position in which it is planted.

When Eothen was built over sixty years ago some young trees were planted right on the edge of the cliff, with no protection whatever from the full fury of the North winds and sea spray, but they defied the elements and still remain silent witnesses to the possibility of tree-growing even in Newquay.

Someone may be inclined to ask why tree planting was neglected in the building of the modern town.   To understand this the conditions that confronted those interested in the welfare of the place at that time must be taken into account.   The first misfortune was the failure of the pilchards to frequent our coast ;   hence the collapse of that industry.   Then the price of coal so increased that the mines which were barely paying their way before had to close down. This brought on the shipping crisis ;   thus the combined failure of those two industries was the means of closing the three ship-building yards, and so the town was left as it were at the parting of the ways.

Fortunately, at that time, the town was becoming more widely known as a health resort. But to adjust matters of town management to the new conditions was a herculean task. The water question had to be faced, as all the wells were on private property with the exception of the one in the Central Square. The houses were small and the number and accommodation inadequate to the demands. A new drainage system had to be carried through, which meant a great outlay. This and the widening of the streets met with much opposition from some of the landowners. They were neither willing to give or even to sell at a reasonable price. There were at that time four natives who stood out as pioneers in this undertaking—Richard Carne, William Michell, John Ennor, and James Pearce. The influence they exerted over their fellow townsmen was wonderful, both in the Council Chamber and out. More than this, they accomplished what hey set out to do and laid the foundation for the greater improvements which are still in progress.

Taking into account the work they did in a few years one can see there would be little time to devote to the decorative side of town planning, but now, with more leisure at their disposal, our leading men might do something to lend shelter by planting trees, and so break the monotony in the appearance of some of the bare-looking rows of houses as they must now seem to those visiting the town for the first time.

CHAPTER **XXIV.**

CONCLUSION.

THE modern idea that Newquay was a name given to
the town in the nineteenth century is a mistake.
The name Towan Blistra applies only to the Beacon and
Headland beyond the Red Lion, but on the town side it was
Newquay with various spellings according to different periods.

In the reign of Henry VI. there is an extract from the
Parochial History thus—" An indulgence was granted by
Edmund Lacy, Bishop of Exeter, January 10th, 1439 for
the construction repair and maintenance of a place called
Key, situated on the sea shore *near* Tewen Blustey."

The fact of the inhabitants asking for an indulgence
shows clearly there was an old Quay here that had fallen
into disrepair even at that early date. Then Carew, the
Cornish historian, writing in 1602, in Queen Elizabeth's
reign, says—" Neither may I omit Newkaye, a place in the
north coast of this Hundred, so called because in *former
times* the inhabitants attempted to remedy a natural defect
by art, which conceit they still possess, though lack of means
among themselves or in the place has left the result in nubibus,
and only left them the benefit of lester-cocks and fisher-
boats."

The " hundred," a division of the county in which
Newquay is situated, is called the Pydar Hundred. " Conceit " is an old term for a fancy or exaggerated notion. In
nubibus means " in the clouds "—a term for an inflated idea.
Lester-cocks is a genus of web-footed birds, including the
skua-gull. So Newquay was left, according to Carew, to
gulls and fishing boats.

Then in the reign of James I., 1615, Thomas Stuer,
who must have been Lord of the Manor, applied for leave to
erect a Pier, so that we see in three reigns the old inhabitants
of Newquay were persistent in asking help from the Govern-

ment, only to meet with disappointment. Carew says " in former times " the inhabitants attempted to build a pier. It is evident that four hundred years before Lomax began, and Treffry finished,the South Pier to its present length, there must have been an arm extending some distance out from some part of the cliff. To see the deserted harbour now it is difficult to realize that in 1889 one hundred and seven ships sailed in and out and that the imports for the year were 9,000 tons, and exports 5,500 tons. Seventy families, fathers and sons, were engaged in the shipping trade then. At one time there were twelve vessels in the harbour. There must have been through the year an average of over four a week, either coming in, or going out. I am inclined to the idea of a succession of Newquays. There is abundant evidence of a town there long before the blown sand from Fistral swept across the fields to the town bay. When the masons in 1852 were excavating in Wesley Hill for the site of the Wesleyan Chapel, and were fifteen feet below the surface they came down on bricks built up that looked like the chimneys of buried houses.

When Augustine Chudleigh, Esq., was carrying out one of his investigations in the interests of archaeology on the West side of Newquay he came across beds of mussel shells about two feet below the surface. The hard periwinkles (locally known as rinkles) were all broken, while the fragile mussel shells were entire. He supposed it was the remains of a shell-fish feast. From the rinkles being broken it is clear that they had no darning needles in those far-off days to extract the body of the creature !

Again, when blown sand was taken out for the foundations of the cottages just under the path leading to the Baptist Chapel, loads of mussel shells were carted away as well as blown sand. Evidently shell-fish was a staple food in those days. Since 1900 there have been evidences to show, during excavations, that the tract of land from the cemetery down to the railway crossing was used as a common burial ground, and very likely from the fragments of weapons and implements that have been found it must have dated back to the Neolithic or New Stone Age. The ruins of an old village could be traced seventy years ago. On the space partially occupied by the Post Office—from Hawke's to Whitehouse's shop, there were the ruins of an old farm house surrounded by the mowey. We often played there as children and always spoke of it as the " old mowey." There were the ruins of a row of houses, where, later, the terrace below the old church was built. I remember one of the old houses was spoken of as the public bakehouse. Another ruin was in a large garden occupying all the space take up now by Jenkins' Stores and yard. One wall was standing when I was a child and it gave me the impression of being a very large house. All those houses must have been hundreds of years old when they fell into decay before the Newquay of my childhood was built.

In 1846 there were 192 houses inhabited and of those only twenty were thatched. Apart from the houses in Deer Park, I don't suppose there are twenty houses of the town of 1846 which are standing now. They have either been pulled down or incorporated into larger buildings.

As the number of visitors increased each summer and others came to reside permanently, criticism was rife concerning the narrow streets and the irregularly built houses. Some of us have watched the new developments, as estates have been purchased, and syndicates formed, and hoped to see great things accomplished, but alas! the hope has not yet been realised. There was a splendid opportunity for town planning when the Island Estate was purchased for building. A magnificent crescent could have been laid out, far back on the estate, with gardens sloping down to the cliff,where an unsurpassed view of coast line and ocean could have been obtained from every house, a decided improvement on the present chaos. Standing by the flagstaff outside the Red Lion Hotel, and looking across to the estate, one cannot fail to be filled with regret at the lost opportunity for artistic laying out of the grounds.

A similar mistake was made when the fields between Lehenver Road and Crantock Street were taken over for building purposes. What a charming view could have been obtained if two terraces from the cemetery to " Evening Side " had been built with gardens between on the slope! All the houses would then have had a splendid view out over the bay.

All the blame for the present lack of plan must not be allowed to fall on the shoulders of the builders, as all plans must receive the approval of the Council.

I know it is easy to criticize, but in future when new land is taken for building, if a little forethought is exercised, much can be accomplished. I am fully persuaded that Newquay has not yet reached the zenith of its prosperity as a watering place, and it rests with the present and future inhabitants to make this an accomplished fact.

APPENDIX.

BILL OF SALE OF TOWAN BLYSTRA.

PLANS and Particulars of the Desirable Manor of Towan
Blystra with the Tolls, payable at the Pier of Newquay
situated in the Parishes of St. Columb Minor and Crantock
in the County of Cornwall ; and the Mineral Dues arising
from the Newquay Silver and Lead Mines, late the property
of Richard Lomax, Esq., for sale by Auction by Mr. Tippett,
at the Red Lion Hotel, Truro, on Thursday, the 25th day
of October, 1838, at 3 o'clock in the afternoon.

The Solicitors are Hodge and Hockin, Truro.   Printed by
W. Pollyblank, St. Nicholas Street, Truro.

Observations :—

This Manor comprises nearly the whole of the flourishing
town of Newquay, together with upwards of 100 acres of
rich and fertile Orchard,   Arable, Meadow and Pasture
land in a high state of cultivation, and 70 acres of valuable
sheep walk, which might, from the facilities afforded by its
contiguity to the sea for producing seaweed and manure,
be converted at a moderate sum into Arable land.   Newquay
is situated on the Northern coast of Cornwall in a fine, open
bay, called Towan Bay, being distant about 12 miles from
Truro and six from St. Columb.   The adjacent coast is
rocky and dangerous and affords no nearer shelter for vessels
or boats than St. Ives, on the one side, and Padstow on the
other.

The late public-spirited proprietor recently erected a
most commodious pier (South) there, capable of receiving
vessels of 700 tons burthen, at an expense exceeding £10,000.
The Pilchard Fishery has been for many years successfully
carried on at this place, and a sum of one shilling per hogshead
on all fish, and a like duty per ton on all imports and exports
is payable to the Lord of the Manor, being secured by an

Act of Parliament passed in the Spring Session of 1838.
The pier dues are now estimated at £190 per annum.

A Railway from Newquay to Tresillian Bridge and from
thence to Truro has been lately projected ; its utility and
advantages are obvious to all persons acquainted with the
locality and its feasability is admitted by all practical men.
It would unite the Northern and Southern Channels and
render a voyage round the Land's End unnecessary. The
various advantages which must accrue to the Lord of the
Manor from this railway cannot be too highly estimated,as the
Pier Dues alone would realize £1500 a year,whilst the rental
arising from the land and houses now in possession (exceeding
£400 per annum) would be proportionately increased.

Valuable lodes of Silver and Lead intersect the Manor.
One valuable mine,called Newquay Silver and Lead Mine,
is now in course of working with good prospects, and it is
distant only five miles from the celebrated Lead and Silver
mine of " East Wheal Rose," whence the late Sir Christopher
Hawkins, Bart., obtained such immense profits and there
is every reason to believe that this mine will be equally
productive. The Harbour Dues and Minerals taken in
conjunction with the lodes in possession and let at convention-
ary Rents form together a property well worthy the attention of capitalists.

Names of the people who were in possession of the houses
and land at the time of the sale (1838) either on lives or terms
of 99 years or otherwise :—

LENGTH OF TIME & DATE OF LEASE.

Tenement.	Time.	Tenant.	Measurement.		
			A.	R.	P.
Parts of Mitchells on which an Inn is					
erected	14 yrs.	Stephen Hoare	5	0	0
Inclosure and Sheepwalk (Fistral) ..	,,	Robert Hawke	70	0	0
Public House, etc., Old Inn	21 yrs.	Wm. Parkyn		1	0
Dwelling houses and gardens occupied					
by Coastguards	60 yrs.	Com.H.M.Customs	20	0	0

Wharfe within the Pier unoccupied ..	—	—		—
Rowley's Tenement House	—	—		—
Orchard and Meadows	14 yrs.	Robert House	4 0	0
Part of Varcoes, Tenement Land ..	,,	Richard Hicks	6 3	0
Part of Varcoes, Tenement Land ..	,,	Wm. Gummoe	5 0	0
Tenement in Carne Lane	,,	Constantine House	6 2	0
Tenement, Lehenvers Lane	,,	John Mitchell	6 0	0
Part of Varcoes & Lehenver's Lane ..	14 yrs.	Geo. Burt	4 0	0
Three Meadows	,,	Mrs. Thomas	4 0	0
Smith's Shop	,,	James Jolly		
House	yearly	Richard Ellery		
Mitchell's Tenement Land	,,	Richard Billing	4 0	0
Bark House	,,	John Stevens & Co.		2
New Enclosure	,,	Wm. Gummoe	1 2	0
House	,,	Grace Burt		4
House part of Blackmore's Ten.	,,	Richard Phillips		
Field	,,	John Hore	2	0
House	,,	James Jolly		
House	,,	Pascoe		
House, part of Blackmore's Ten.	,,	Mary Clemow		
New Enclosure Garden (boat bdg). ..	,,	Thomas Clemens		
Garden on the Common	,,	Wm. Green		
New Enclosure	,,	Stephen Dark		
Acknowledgment for Wesley Ch... ..	,,	Wm. Hocking		
Garden extending from Fore Street to				
Baptist Chapel	,,	Richard Carne		
Dwelling House, Quay Cellars, Malt-		Representatives of		
house and land	99 yrs.	J. Bennettoe	6 0	0
James' Ten., Dwelling Ho. & Land ..	,,	John Carrivick	7 2	0
Dwelling House and Meadows	,,	Rep. of J. Bennettoe	2 0	0
House and Garden	,,	Wm. Hocking		12
Rose Cellars, House and Meadow.. ..	,,	Richard Billing	1 0	0
House and Garden	,,	Wm. Billing		
,, ,, ,, ...	,,	Rep. of W. Harris		

,, ,, ,, ...	,,	,, E. Eddyvean
Land	,,	Wm. Clemens
House and Garden	,,	Ann Glanville
,, ,,..	,,	John Giles
,, ,,..	,,	Robert Sleeman
,, ,, ...	,,	Wm. Trebilcock
Cellar and Garden	,,	John Wilton
Ten. of Towan House and Garden ..	,,	John Clemens
House and Garden	,,	Mary Sleeman 8
Towan Island	,,	Wm. Billing 6
Fly Cellars	,,	Norway & Co.
New Enclosure	,,	Richard Billing 7 2 0
New Enclosure (Tower)	,,	Fredk.Rogers,Esq. 4 2 0
Part of Marshall's Meadow	,,	Wm. Barry
New Enclosure on which two houses are erected	,,	John Mitchell 2 18
New Enclosure	,,	Richard Hicks 2 0 39
,, ...	,,	Matthew Knight 2 3 5
,, ...	,,	Robert Sleeman 2 3 0
,, ...	,,	Mrs. Thomas 31
Enclosure building ground	,,	George Burt
New Enclosure	,,	Samuel Martyn
,, ...	,,	George Burt
,, ...	,,	R.Crebo &TGarland 27
Part of Marshall's Meadow	,,	Thomas Salmon
House and Garden	,,	Wm. Hocking 14
Waste Plot in which houses and shop ..	,,	J. Cardell, Esq.
New Enclosure	,,	Wm. Tuman
,, ...	,,	Thomas Moses 22
,, on which is house	,,	Mrs.Mountstevens
,, ,, ...	,,	Wm. Carrivick 15
Garden and House	,,	Matthew Knight 11
New Enclosure	,,	Mrs. Thomas 1 1 8
,, ,, ...	,,	Richard Stephens 1 1 0

Towan Hd. Spy Cellars and Land ..	42 yrs.	Norway & Co.	5 0 0
Dwelling House and garden	99 yrs.	Frank Roberts	
New Enclosure	,,	Johnson Hicks	
,, ...	,,	Rich. Hocking (jnr.)	20
Part of Common	,,	John Wilton	1 0 0
New Enclosure on which is house ..	,,	Richard Hicks	
New Enclosure	,,	James Matthew	18
Waste Plot	,,	J. Cardell, Esq.	
New Enclosure	,,	Richard Tumon	
Part of the Common	,,	John Carter	16
New Enclosure	,,	James Clemens	2
,, ,, from Common	,,	Thomas Teague	11
House	,,	Rich. Trebilcock	
New Enclosure	,,	Wm. Clemens	1 0
,, ...	,,	Enoder Billing	10
,, ...	,,	Thomas Osborne	18
Plot of Land	,,	John Cardell, Esq.	6
New Enclosure	,,	Wm. Trebilcock	15
Garden	,,	Richard Hocking	4
Plot of Land	,,	Silas Tinny	3
Acknowledgment of Road	,,	Wm. Trebilcock	
Acknowledgment of Pigstye	,,	Wm. Clemens	
Waste of Piece Sett to search for minerals	,,	Messrs. Mitchell	18

THE END.

Marlborough:
Printed at the "Times" Offices,
1923.